INSTITUTE OF LEADERSHIP & MANAGEMENT

SUPERSERIES

Managing
Lawfully –
Health,
Safety and
Environment

FOURTH EDITION

Pergamon
Flexible
Learning

Published for the
Institute of Leadership & Management by

AMSTERDAM BOSTON HEIDELBERG LONDON NEW YORK OXFORD
PARIS SAN DIEGO SAN FRANCISCO SINGAPORE SYDNEY TOKYO

Pergamon Flexible Learning
An imprint of Elsevier
Linacre House, Jordan Hill, Oxford OX2 8DP
30 Corporate Drive, Burlington, MA 01803

First published 1986
Second edition 1991
Third edition 1997
Fourth edition 2003
Reprinted 2005

British Library Cataloguing in Publication Data
A catalogue record for this book is available from the British Library

ISBN 0 7506 5841 X

For information on Pergamon Flexible Learning
visit our website at www.bh.com/pergamonfl

Institute of Leadership & Management
registered office
1 Giltspur Street
London
EC1A 9DD
Telephone 020 7294 3053
www.i-l-m.com
ILM is part of the City & Guilds Group

Working together to grow
libraries in developing countries

www.elsevier.com | www.bookaid.org | www.sabre.org

ELSEVIER   BOOK AID International   Sabre Foundation

Authors: Joe Johnson, Colin Everson and Dela Jenkins
Editor: Dela Jenkins
Editorial management: Genesys, www.genesys-consultants.com
Based on previous material by: Joe Johnson
Composition by Genesis Typesetting, Rochester, Kent
Printed and bound in China

Contents

Contents

Workbook introduction

1 ILM Super Series study links

This workbook addresses the issues of *Managing Lawfully – Health, Safety and Environment*. Should you wish to extend your study to other Super Series workbooks covering related or different subject areas, you will find a comprehensive list at the back of this book.

2 Links to ILM Qualifications

This workbook relates to the following learning outcomes in segments from the ILM Level 3 Introductory Certificate in First Line Management and the Level 3 Certificate in First Line Management.

C5.3 Health and Safety – Law and Practice
  1 Identify significant legislation related to health, safety and welfare at work
  2 Explain how the law affects both the first line manager and the work team members and the duties it imposes
  3 Identify the main features of an organization's Health and Safety Policy
  4 Understand the concept of a Competent Person and the need to train employees in health and safety
  5 Identify appropriate procedures for dealing with injuries, diseases and dangerous occurrences.

C5.7 The Environment
1 Understand the potential risks to the environment from business operations
2 List the main areas covered by environmental legislation
3 Contribute to reducing the effects on the environment by closely monitoring operations in accordance with organizational policies and procedures.

3 Links to S/NVQs in Management

This workbook relates to the following element of the Management Standards that are used in S/NVQs in Management, as well as a range of other S/NVQs.

A1.2 Maintain healthy, safe and productive work conditions.

It will also help you to develop the following Personal Competences:

- building teams
- focusing on results
- thinking and taking decisions.

4 Workbook objectives

All managers need to know enough to ensure that the work activities they control remain within the requirements of the law. In the areas of health, safety and the environment, this is becoming increasingly difficult, because so many changes in the law have been made in recent times. Unfortunately, ignorance of the law is no defence, so it's of no avail to plead 'Nobody told me!'

As a first line manager, you should make it your job to learn as much about the law as you can, even if only to help you in planning your team's work.

Also, as a team leader, you have special responsibilities for the health and safety of your team members, as well as your own. Another good reason for studying the law on health and safety is that it provides guidance on minimum standards.

If you need one further reason for reading about the law, it is this. If you break the law, **there is a real possibility that action could be taken against you, personally, as well as against your organization**. This is especially likely to happen if a serious accident occurs as a result of your actions, or because of your failure to act.

This workbook is divided into three sessions. Sessions A and B are devoted to health and safety aspects of the law, and Session C is concerned with the environment.

In Session A you will be able to read about the background to the law on health and safety. Session B goes on to describe the principal Acts and Regulations.

Session C explains environmental law in terms of its sources, its history and the way that it is enforced, and summarizes the main statutes related to the environment.

Notes on studying this workbook.

This book contains quite a lot of detail about health and safety and environmental legislation. **You are not expected to remember it all.** The best way to tackle the workbook is to read it through, completing the activities, and answering the self-assessment questions, in the usual way. You should be able to follow the points made, but don't feel you have to learn them all by heart.

Whenever you come across areas of law that seem particularly relevant to you and your job, make a note to remind yourself to find out more. There is a list of extensions at the back of the book, on pages 98–101; alternatively, there may be people in your organization who can give you guidance.

4.1 Objectives

When you have completed this workbook you will be better able to:

■   identify the most important laws related to health and safety;
■   find out more about laws that are especially relevant to the work you do;

- explain to your team how the law affects them, and the duties imposed by the law on everyone at work;
- understand the law on the environment.

5 Activity planner

The following Activities require some planning so you may want to look at these now.

- In Activity 4 you are asked to extract information from your organization's Health and Safety Policy.
- In Activity 13 you are asked to think about the way you give information about health and safety to your team at present, and how you might improve your effectiveness in this respect.
- Activity 22 asks you to find a data sheet relating to a hazardous substance in your department.
- For Activity 24, you are expected to look at the training you give on hazardous substances in your work area.

Some or all of these Activities may provide the basis of evidence for your S/NVQ portfolio. All Portfolio Activities and the Work-based assignment are signposted with this icon.

The icon states the elements to which the portfolio activities and Work-based assignment relate.

In the Work-based assignment you are required to investigate how well your part of the organization complies with one of the sets of regulations we discuss.

Session A
Background to health and safety legislation

1 Introduction

Until well into the twentieth century, serious accidents and occupational hazards leading to disease were a normal part of working life for millions of the working population. People were made deaf by excessive noise in mills, burned by slag and molten metal in foundries, their lungs wrecked by dust in mining and farming, their organs poisoned by lead in paints or mercury used in making hats.

Many large rivers were so polluted that nothing could live in them. Air pollution, much of it from domestic chimneys, led to hundreds of deaths every year and illness for countless other people. 'Smogs' in London and most other towns and cities continued into the 1950s, bringing death and respiratory diseases to large numbers of people.

Standards have improved immensely since 1974. The point has now been reached where each successive improvement is harder to attain at affordable cost.

Laws to regulate working conditions began to be introduced in the nineteenth century. They tackled only the worst abuses, such as child labour and the employment of women and children in horrific conditions underground in mines.

Parliament finally did something about the state of the nineteenth century Thames when the stench became so unbearable that it was impossible to open windows. Thus the London sewerage system, which was still used well into the twentieth century, was built to assuage the discomfort of Members of Parliament.

Until the mid twentieth century, the health and safety of people at work continued to be poorly protected. Legislation was piecemeal, often following specific abuses or disasters.

1.1 The Health & Safety At Work, etc. Act 1974

The major turning point came in 1974, with the first comprehensive Health & Safety at Work, etc. Act (HSWA), which imposed a general duty of care on virtually every employer.

The Act imposes clear duties on employers relating to health, safety and welfare at work, and also provides guidance on how to promote high standards in these areas. It also imposes obligations on employees to take care for themselves and others who may be affected by their actions.

The opening sentence of the Act includes the word 'welfare':

> 'An Act to make further provision for securing the health, safety and *welfare* of persons at work . . .'

and it is important to keep this third aspect of the Act in mind when you are looking at health and safety issues at your workplace.

But we begin with a preface to our subject.

2 Introduction to health and safety legislation

We need to start by seeing health and safety in the context of the law in general.

2.1 Sources of law

The law applicable in the UK is derived from three principal sources:

■ **statute law**

Acts of parliament, such as the Health and Safety at Work, etc. Act 1974, together with subordinate legislation (sometimes called 'statutory instruments'), such as the Management of Health and Safety at Work Regulations 1999.

■ **common law**

based on case law – the decisions made in courts over the centuries. Once a judgment is made, a **precedent** is established. A court is bound to follow earlier decisions made in higher courts, or in courts at the same level.

■ **contract law**

governing agreements between two parties. Contract law does not play much part in health and safety.

Most health and safety law has been created through statute law.

Under common law, an action might be brought for the tort of 'negligence', which may be defined as:

> 'the omission to do something which a reasonable person would do, or doing something which a prudent or reasonable person would not do'.

To prove negligence, the injured party, or plaintiff, must prove that:

■ a duty of care existed on the part of the defendant towards the plaintiff;
■ the defendant has breached that duty by behaving in a way in which a reasonable person would not behave;
■ the plaintiff must have suffered some damage.

2.2 Civil law and criminal law

Both criminal law and civil law are important to organizations in terms of health and safety.

Anyone committing a crime has offended against the State, and is in breach of criminal law. If an organization fails to comply with its statutory health and safety duties, then it or its officers may be prosecuted under criminal law. If guilt is proved 'beyond reasonable doubt', the offender may be punished by the court by having a fine imposed. In theory at least, jail sentences can also be passed on individuals.

Under civil actions, a plaintiff sues a defendant, usually for damages, that is, financial compensation. As an example, an individual may sue an employer if he or she is injured at work. A lesser standard of proof applies in civil actions than in criminal prosecutions: cases have to be proved 'on the balance of probabilities', rather than 'beyond reasonable doubt'.

Activity 1

2 mins

Briefly describe the **two** main ways in which organizations may have legal actions brought as a result of an accident at work.

_____

_____

_____

_____

The following diagram shows the possible routes that could be taken through the legal system, following an accident at work.

The two main routes are through the civil and criminal courts. The third route, shown on the right of the diagram, is via an employment tribunal.

EXTENSION 1
This table is taken from
Health and Safety Law by
Jeremy Stranks.

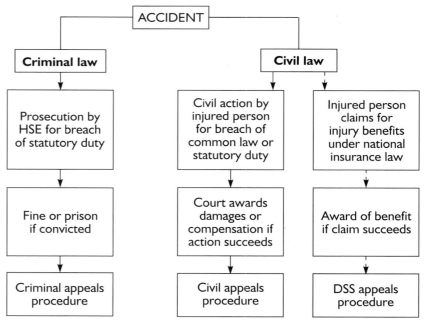

Redrawn, with kind permission, from a diagram in _Health and Safety Law_, by Jeremy Stranks

2.3 European law

The United Kingdom is a member State of the European Union (EU), along with 14 other nations: Austria, Belgium, Denmark, Finland, France, Germany, Greece, Holland, Ireland, Italy, Luxembourg, Portugal, Spain and Sweden.

Although we still make our own laws in the UK, membership of the EU has had a profound effect on our laws and lawmaking. One important fact is that, if ever there is any conflict, European laws take precedence over national laws in the courts.

The two principal instruments by which the European Union makes laws are:

- **EU Regulations** that apply directly in all member countries. Actions based on EU Regulations can be brought in national courts. (EU Regulations should not be confused with UK Regulations, many of which we will discuss in this workbook.)
- **Directives**, which bind member countries to comply with an agreed ruling. Unlike EU Regulations, Directives are normally made into national laws by each State. A good deal of modern health and safety legislation is the direct result of EU Directives.

The **Single European Act** was made law at the beginning of 1993. Its aim is to eliminate technical barriers to trade by introducing a new approach to technical harmonization and standards. Largely as a result of this Act, national standards for health and safety within the Union are being made to conform with one another.

Much of the environmental law either proposed or already in force stems from the European Union.

2.4 Approved codes of practice and guidance notes

These two kinds of document are useful sources of information about the law.

Approved Codes of Practice (ACOPs) are issued by the Health and Safety Commission (HSC) as interpretations of Regulations, and are intended to help people apply the law in practice. ACOPs are designed to:

- make Regulations more plain or more specific;
- explain how Regulations can be complied with in a satisfactory way.

Example

Regulation 15 of the Workplace (Health, Safety and Welfare) Regulations 1992 states that:

1   No window, skylight or ventilator which is capable of being opened shall be likely to be opened, closed or adjusted in a manner which exposes any person performing such operation to a risk to his health or safety.

2   No window, skylight or ventilator shall be in a position when open which is likely to expose any person in the workplace to a risk to his health or safety.

Part of the ACOP for this regulation says:

153 It should be possible to reach and operate the control of openable windows, skylights and ventilators in a safe manner. Where necessary, window poles or similar equipment should be kept available, or a stable platform or other safe means of access should be provided. Controls should be so placed that people are not likely to fall through or out of the window. Where there is a danger of falling from a height, devices should be provided to prevent the window opening too far.

Guidance notes may also be issued, either by the Health and Safety Commission (HSC) or the Health and Safety Executive (HSE). They include, for example, advice on action to be taken by employers in order to conform with the law.

To summarize this introduction:

■ the three sources of law are statute law, common law and contract law;
■ it's important to distinguish between criminal law and civil law, and there is a separate court system for each; however, both are important in health and safety;
■ the UK's membership of the European Union has had a profound effect on our environmental, health and safety legislation;
■ useful documents that are intended to help people apply the law are Approved Codes of Practice (ACOPs) and guidance notes.

3 The Health and Safety at Work, etc. Act, 1974 (HSWA)

EXTENSION 2
Workplace health, safety and welfare: a short guide for managers is available from HSE Books.

The Health and Safety at Work, etc. Act 1974 (HSWA) is the most important safety legislation ever to come into force in the UK. It is an 'enabling' Act which 'enables' Ministers (that is gives them the power) to introduce Regulations, called 'Statutory Instruments' and 'Approved Codes of Practice' (ACOPs) which explain in far more detail how the general provisions of the Act are to be implemented. While the enabling Act itself does not need to be changed or updated except in extremely unusual circumstances, Ministers can update Regulations and ACOPs that have been created under the Act whenever they think it necessary. These Regulations and ACOPs are discussed in detail in Session B.

Under HSWA, three separate bodies exist to promote health, safety and welfare on a continuing basis. These bodies are the HSC, HSE and EMAS.

3.1 Health and Safety Commission (HSC)

The Health and Safety Commission (HSC) is a body that includes representatives from all interested parties, including industry and the trades unions, under a 'chair' appointed by the Secretary of State. The Commission advises the Government on long-term issues and makes strategic recommendations for the continuous improvement of standards.

The HSC publishes comprehensive data every year, available from HSE Books.

3.2 Health and Safety Executive (HSE)

The Health and Safety Executive (HSE) is charged with enforcing the law through its inspectors, who have wide powers to investigate incidents and accidents and who can serve prohibition orders and enforcement notices on defaulting organizations. Local authorities also have responsibility for some aspects of enforcement.

The HSE's role in accident reporting and investigation – the 'RIDDOR' Regulations

If an organization's health and safety standards are to be continuously imposed, it is essential for them to have accurate, up-to-date information on incidents and accidents that have occurred. The UK's data are as good as any in the world and are obtained under the Reporting of Injuries, Diseases and Dangerous Occurrences Regulations of 1995 (RIDDOR).

The Regulations demand that a 'responsible person', normally the person in control of the afflicted site, reports what has happened on a prescribed form to the HSE or, sometimes, to the Local Authority.

Safety representatives have a statutory right to review these reports and to investigate the circumstances. In Session B you will find details of the categories that must be reported and that form the basis for statistics published by the HSC. Safety Committees will consider such reports as a standing item on their agendas.

3.3 Employment Medical Advisory Service (EMAS)

The Employment Medical Advisory Service (EMAS) provides information and advice to the Government, employers and employees on medical matters affecting employment.

Activity 2 · 2 mins

Who in law do you think would have duties under HSWA?

_____

_____

_____

Both employers and employees have duties under HSWA.

Let's look at the duties of the employer first.

3.4 The employer's overall duties under HSWA

Under HSWA, an employer has a duty:

> 'to ensure, as far as reasonably practicable, the health, safety and welfare at work of all his employees'.

We will discuss what 'as far as reasonably practicable' means in the next section.

The key words in the extract are '**as far as reasonably practicable**'. This is the 'yardstick' by which an employer's actions will be judged.

To do this, the employer will need to be sure that (to give a few examples):

- plant and equipment are safely installed, operated and maintained;
- systems of work are checked frequently, to ensure that risks from hazards are minimized;
- the work environment is regularly monitored to ensure that people are protected from any toxic contaminants;
- safety equipment is inspected regularly;
- risks to health from natural and artificial substances are minimized.

HSWA also places an obligation on employers to take care of the health and safety of non-employees.

Activity 3

3 mins

Can you suggest **two** groups of people, other than employees, that an employer may have duties towards under health and safety laws?

_____

_____

_____

_____

_____

You may have mentioned:

- self-employed people or contractors' employees working on site;
- customers who visit (for instance) shop or garage premises;
- visiting suppliers;
- other visitors;
- the general public living and working outside the worksite.

3.5 Health & Safety Policy Statement

The HSWA requires all employers with five or more employees to prepare, publish and keep up to date a statement of the organization's general policy towards health and safety at work.

The clear intention is that the Policy as set out is a practical document that will ensure that there is a 'progressive improvement in health and safety performance' (Management of Health and Safety at Work Regulations, approved Code of Practice). The requirements are as follows.

General Policy Statement

This must:

- **state clearly** what the organization's policy is, for example 'to protect the health, safety and welfare of all employees, contractors, visitors and customers while they are at work or on its premises'. Account may also need to be taken of neighbouring sites that may be affected by the organisation's activities;
- **require acceptance** of the Policy by all personnel, including acceptance of the need for safety training;
- **commit** the organization to improving safety performance continuously.

Organisation and arrangements

These need to:

- **identify specifically** the responsibilities of office holders, such as the chief executive and other executives, and specialist advisors, such as safety officers and occupational health professionals;
- **specify resources** that will be provided to implement the policy, including those required for systematic training of personnel;
- **state** who is responsible for publishing the policy and keeping it up to date.

Activity 4

10 mins

S/NVQ A1.2

Obtain a copy of your own organization's Health and Safety Policy. Compare it with the general requirements indicated here and then use it to answer the following questions.

In your organization, who is responsible for issuing the Policy?

_____

Who is responsible for providing resources to implement it?

_____

What responsibilities are assigned to all general employees?

_____

What mention is made of visitors, contractors' employees, customers and neighbouring sites?

_____

If you have any problem obtaining the Policy Statement or obtaining the information, please talk to your manager.

3.6 The employee's duties under HSWA

Under HSWA, employees have a duty:

- to take reasonable care to avoid injury to themselves or to others by their work activities;
- to co-operate with employers and others in meeting the requirements of the law including the acceptance of health and safety training; and
- not to interfere with or misuse anything provided to protect their health, safety and welfare.

Activity 5 · 6 mins

Kenny works for a contractor who is replacing paving slabs and kerbstones in a busy market place. He has to cut the slabs using power tools, which create dust and noise. The work must be carried out while the market is working and in all weathers. His work mates and many members of the public are likely to be in the general area as well.

Kenny's employer has a duty to do everything 'which is reasonably practicable' to ensure his safety. But what steps should Kenny take to ensure the safety of:

■ himself;
■ his working colleagues;
■ the general public.

Kenny

_____

_____

His working colleagues

_____

_____

The general public

_____

_____

The list of items you have noted will probably include the following:

To ensure his safety, Kenny should:

■ wear all protective clothing as he is trained and instructed to do, including ear defenders, eye protection and safety footwear;
■ check equipment and use it only if it is in safe working condition and he is trained and authorized to use it;
■ use equipment only for the purpose intended, and using all the guards, noise and dust control devices specified;
■ take account of weather and site conditions.

To ensure the safety of his working colleagues, Kenny should:

- check that they will not be adversely affected by noise, dust or fumes;
- store materials and offcuts safely, to ensure that he does not create tripping hazards;
- position any designated safety barriers as required and work within them.

To ensure the safety of the general public, Kenny should:

- take the same safety measures as for his colleagues;
- remember that certain people, such as children and the elderly, may not be aware of hazards, and that they do not have ear defenders, etc. provided to them;
- ensure that his work is confined by safety barriers and that the public is protected from dust, flying particles and excessive noise.

Activity 6

4 mins

Jot down **three** things you would expect a member of **your** team to do, or **not** do, in order to help ensure the safety of others.

_____

_____

_____

_____

Your response will be relevant to the kind of job you do. In general, you might expect a team member:

- to think of the safety and health of others when carrying out his or her job

For example, Kenny would be expected to protect his workmates and members of the general public from the noise, dust and fumes he will create. In another kind of job, a typist in an office would be expected to make sure that cables, boxes and other obstacles are not a hazard to people walking by.

■ **to behave sensibly and responsibly in matters of health and safety**

For instance, it would be irresponsible for someone to cover up a safety notice, or to use a fire bucket for another purpose, or to prop open a fire door that should be kept closed.

■ **not to indulge in 'horseplay' or practical jokes**

The team leader sometimes has to take care that a 'harmless bit of fun' is not allowed to turn into something more dangerous. A good leader will make plain what is allowed and what isn't.

■ **to obey the rules of the organization**

People tend to break safety rules for many reasons. For example, because:

■ they aren't aware of the rules;
■ they don't see any point in the rules;
■ the rules impose conflicting restrictions, such as slowing down a process which the person wants to complete as quickly as possible: there is often a great temptation to 'cut corners';
■ they see other people, such as managers and external contractors, ignoring the rules, and follow their bad example.

Activity 7 · 3 mins

Can you think of an instance where someone in your team has been tempted to cut corners in a job, and thereby has compromised safety? If so, describe it briefly.

_____

_____

_____

_____

_____

_____

Depending on the kind of work you are in, you may have suggested some of the following.

- Not bothering to put on protective clothing.

  'I know I should have worn a safety helmet, but I was only going to be out in the yard for two minutes. How was I to know that it would be slippery and that I would fall and crack my head open?' (Man speaking from hospital bed.)

- Not using the right equipment.

  'The step ladder was in use at the time, and I only wanted one item from the top shelf to finish the whole job. Now it looks like I'll be off work for three months.' (Woman on crutches.)

- Not isolating equipment before working on it.

  'Yes, I admit that I should have checked that the electrical power was off before I asked young Peter to open the fuse-box. I was thinking about how much time the interruption was costing us. Now I'll have to live with this for the rest of my life.' (Supervisor at inquiry into fatal accident.)

- Working on, knowing the risks, and choosing to ignore them for one reason or another.

  'The only way to get to the lift control box is to stick your head into the shaft. I suppose we should have shut down the system – but we'd been told that two people were trapped in the lift between floors. We've never had an accident till now. It was a succession of events that caused it. First of all the lift wasn't faulty at all – it was just that one of the doors wasn't shut properly. The trapped people got out, but no one told us. Then someone must have knocked down the warning notice on the ground floor, and somebody else used the lift just at the time Jim was leaning into the shaft. He didn't stand a chance when that balancing weight came down.' (Maintenance engineer talking after fatal accident.)

To sum up:

- Employees have responsibilities under HSWA:

  - to take care for their own health and safety, and that of their colleagues;
  - to co-operate in meeting the requirements of the law;
  - not to interfere with or misuse anything provided to protect their health, safety and welfare.

- People who cut corners endanger themselves and others.

4 Levels of statutory duty

In law, there are three separate levels of statutory duty. From the lowest to the highest, they are:

- ■ 'reasonably practicable' requirements;
- ■ 'practicable' requirements;
- ■ 'absolute' requirements.

Let's discuss what each of these means.

4.1 The duty to act in a 'reasonably practicable' manner

You will recall that a key phrase, repeated many times in the Health and Safety at Work, etc. Act 1974, is 'as far as reasonably practicable'.

To illustrate what is 'reasonably practicable' so far as health and safety is concerned, read the following case.

Some new partitions were being erected in an open-plan office by contractors. The work was dusty and noisy, even though it had been screened off. The main route from the office to the cloakrooms and rest room was affected. The remaining passageway was narrow, dark and crossed by trailing leads. Some building materials were being stored 'temporarily' in it.

Several staff complained to their team leader, demanding that she 'do something about it before someone gets hurt'. She replied that 'It's only for a few days' and they 'should just be extra careful'.

Activity 8

4 mins

In your opinion:

■ are the staff's requests for action justified?
■ was their team leader acting in a 'reasonably practicable' way by telling them to ignore the problem because it was 'only for a few days'?

_____

_____

_____

It is reasonable for the staff to complain. Tripping is a major cause of accidents. In a 'few days' it would be quite possible for someone to trip over leads or materials stored in a narrow, dark passage on a busy route. It would be 'reasonably practical' for the team leader, either directly or with help from her manager, to demand that the materials be moved out of the passage, that trailing leads be re-routed safely and that temporary lighting be rigged safely. The cost would be minimal and proportionate to the benefits gained.

This case was perhaps not too difficult to make a judgement about. Other situations may not be so straightforward. The expression 'so far as is reasonably practicable' has only acquired a clear meaning through many interpretations by the courts.

According to the Health and Safety Executive:

EXTENSION 3
This extract and the one below, is from page 30 of _Successful Health and Safety Management_, published by HSE Books.

■ 'To carry out a duty so far as is reasonably practicable means that **the degree of risk** in a particular activity or environment **can be balanced against the time, trouble, cost and physical difficulty of taking measures to avoid the risk**.

■ If these are so disproportionate to the risk that it would be unreasonable for the persons concerned to have to incur them to prevent it, they are not obliged to do so.

■ **The greater the risk the more likely it is that it is reasonable to go to very substantial expense, trouble and invention to reduce it**. But if the consequences and the extent of a risk are small, insistence on great expense would not be considered reasonable.

■ It is important to remember that the judgement is an objective one and **the size or financial position of the employer are immaterial**.'

4.2 'Practicable' requirements

The phrase 'so far as is practicable' – without the qualifying word 'reasonably' – implies a stricter standard. The interpretation of the phrase given by HSE is as follows.

'This term generally embraces **whatever is technically possible** in the light of current knowledge, which the person concerned had, or ought to have had, at the time. The **cost, time, and trouble involved are not to be taken into account**.'

4.3 'Absolute' requirements

In health and safety Regulations, such as those we will discuss in the next section, the words 'shall' or 'must' are used frequently. In these cases, there can be no argument or interpretation: the law **must** be obeyed.

Example

Regulation 7 (page 26) of the Health and Safety (Display Screen Equipment) Regulations 1992 states that:

1 Every employer **shall** ensure that operators and users at work in his undertaking are provided with adequate information about –

   a all aspects of health and safety relating to their workstations; and
   b such measures taken by him in compliance with his duties under regulations 2 and 3 as relate to them and their work.

In brief, for all employers:

- 'reasonably practicable' means that the degree of risk has to be balanced against the cost, time and difficulty of taking measures to avoid the risk;
- 'practicable' means that the cost, time and difficulty are not to be considered – technical feasibility is the only consideration;
- 'absolute' – often indicated by the word 'shall' – means that the law **must** be obeyed.

Before going on to look at how the health and safety law is enforced, you need to be aware of another important Act that is in force in parallel with HSWA. This is the Fire Precautions Act 1971.

5 Fire Precautions Act 1971

This Act governs fire safety at most non-domestic premises in the UK.

The Act's basic requirement is that all premises that meet certain criteria must hold a current Fire Certificate, kept and displayed prominently on the site. Such premises include:

- most hotels and boarding houses;
- offices, shops, factories and railway premises where:
  - more than 20 people work at any one time; or
  - more than ten people are employed at any one time other than on the ground floor; or
  - the premises are part of a larger building which meets either of the first two conditions; or
  - explosives or highly flammable materials are stored or used.

A valid Fire Certificate will specify:

- the use or uses of the site, the means of escape from it (usually indicated on a plan) and how this will be kept usable at all times;
- how a fire may be fought – including sprinkler systems and localized equipment;
- warning systems, emergency and evacuation procedures and training to be given to staff.

6 Enforcing the law

It is the job of the Health and Safety Inspectorate or, in some smaller businesses, Environmental Health Officers, to enforce the law.

Inspectors have wide-reaching powers. These include the right to:

- enter and inspect any premises, at any time, where it is considered that there may be dangers to health or safety;

- be accompanied by any duly authorized person, such as a policeman or a doctor;
- enquire into the circumstances of accidents;
- require that facilities and assistance be provided by anyone able to give them;
- take statements;
- require that areas be left undisturbed;
- collect evidence, take photographs, make measurements, and so on;
- take possession of articles;
- require the production of books and documents.

To enforce certain actions, an inspector can:

- issue a **prohibition notice**, which stops – with immediate effect – people from carrying on activities which are considered to involve a risk of serious personal injury;
- issue an **improvement notice**, which compels an employer to put right conditions that contravene the law, within a specified time period;
- initiate **prosecutions**, especially in the case of repeated, deliberate or severe offences.

It goes without saying that managers are expected to give their full co-operation to the enforcing authorities. The liability for personal prosecutions is very real.

An employer can appeal against an improvement notice or a prohibition notice. Here is an example of the case one company put up against a prohibition notice. The prohibition notice was issued to prevent a cutting machine being used, because a safety guard had been removed.

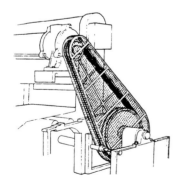

From HSE book *Work Equipment – Guidance on Regulations*, page 56.

The guard was removed to enable the machine to cope with an oversize order which was successfully completed. When the guard was removed the electronic cut-out mechanism, which would normally stop the machine running without the guard, was damaged.

The manufacturers of the electronic components for this type of guard have gone out of business, and it will take some time to find a suitable alternative, although the company is making every effort to do so.

To have a cut-out mechanism made specially would be very expensive.

The company is appealing against the prohibition notice on the grounds of cost and difficulty.

Activity 9

3 mins

Imagine you have to make a judgment on this appeal. You understand that cost and difficulty is an important consideration for any organization, but your main concern is that of safety.

Would you agree that the prohibition should be lifted, given the circumstances? YES/NO

Give a brief reason for your answer.

_____

_____

_____

_____

_____

_____

In spite of the cost and difficulties, there is not sufficient reason to lift the prohibition notice. Safety must come first. If the company were to use the machine without a guard, or with a guard that could be removed easily because there is no cut-out mechanism, someone might be seriously injured.

It is in fact very difficult to make a successful appeal against a prohibition notice or an improvement notice.

7 Safety representatives and committees

Everyone has a part to play in health and safety matters. It seems sensible for an employer, therefore, to encourage employee participation in this area.

EXTENSION 4
If you are interested in this subject, you may want to read the Health and Safety Commission booklet *Safety Representatives and Safety Committees*.

In this section, we'll take a brief look at the role of safety representatives and safety committees in health and safety.

The regulations covering safety representatives and safety committees are included in Section 15 of HSWA and in the Safety Representatives and Safety Committees Regulations 1977.

7.1 The safety representative

A safety representative is someone appointed by a recognized trade union to represent employees on health and safety matters at work. Because they need to be familiar with the hazards of the workplace and the work being done, safety representatives are usually people with two or more years' experience in that particular job.

Safety representatives have three main functions. The first one is to take all reasonably practicable steps to keep themselves informed.

Activity 10 · 4 mins

What kind of information do you think an employees' representative on health and safety would need, in order to do a good job?

_____

_____

_____

_____

Safety representatives would surely need to be familiar with:

- what the law says about the health and safety of people at work, and particularly the people they represent;
- the particular hazards of the workplace;
- the measures needed to eliminate these hazards, or to cut down the risk from them;
- the employer's health and safety policy, and the organization and arrangements for putting that policy into practice.

The second main function is to encourage co-operation between their employer and employees so that:

■ measures can be developed and promoted to ensure the health and safety of employees;
■ the effectiveness of these measures can be checked.

The third function is to bring to the attention of the employer any unsafe or unhealthy conditions or working practices, or unsatisfactory welfare arrangements.

Activity 11

4 mins

Knowing the functions of a safety representative, you may be able to work out the kind of activities involved. Jot down **two** possible activities, if you can.

_____

_____

_____

_____

As you may have mentioned, safety representatives will usually be involved in:

■ talking to employees about particular health and safety problems;
■ carrying out inspections of the workplace to see whether there are any real or potential hazards that haven't been adequately addressed;
■ reporting to employers about these problems and other matters connected to health and safety in that workplace;
■ taking part in accident investigations.

Inspections and reports should be recorded formally in writing.

7.2 Safety committees

An employer is legally obliged to set up a safety committee after receiving written requests to do so from two safety representatives.

It is good practice for **all** employers to operate a safety committee, and nowadays a very large number do, whether or not they have been requested to do so by safety representatives.

Ideally, a site safety committee should comprise:

■ a senior manager for the site who is **not** a safety specialist and who chairs the committee;
■ representatives from all key departments;
■ union safety representatives (where they have been appointed);
■ specialist employees, including engineers, medical staff, risk managers, safety professionals – according to the organization's structure;
■ external specialists and advisors on an 'occasional' basis.

Larger sites may have a number of departmental committees as well as a site committee.

The safety committee:

■ reviews the organization's health and safety rules and procedures;
■ studies statistics and trends of accidents and health problems;
■ considers reports and information received from health and safety inspectors;
■ keeps a watch on the effectiveness of the safety content of employee training.

Let's look at the kind of accident statistics that might typically be collected in an organization.

Activity 12

5 mins

Read through the accident statistics on page 25 and try to spot **three** facts that might be of interest to a safety committee.

_____

_____

_____

_____

_____

Portdown Engineering (Bosham) Ltd.
ACCIDENT STATISTICS SHEET

Period: From 23.03 To 19.04

Date of accident	Length of service	Name, clock no. and department	Sex	Age	Occupation	Description of accident	Nature of injury	Absent (days)	Code
25.03	7 yrs 6 mths	J.P. Peters Blownware Factory	F	41	Inspector	While inspecting glass in the Blownware factory a flask exploded causing injury.	Cut right forearm.	6	1/14
09.04	3 mths	C.K. Rush Packing Dept.	F	22	Packer	While packing glass and using stapler machine she felt pain in her neck.	Pain in neck.	5	14
19.04	4 yrs 10 mths	J.C. Isoz Packer	M	32	Packer	While packing glass he developed pains in both arm and back.	Pain in arms and back.	10	14
26.03	4 yrs 4 mths	S.J. Ruffle Deptford Dec' Cent.	F	43	Packer	While lifting glass from crate she strained her back.	Back strain.	15	5
23.03	1 mth	I.T. Hones Packing Dept.	M	17	Packer	While packing glass, a roll of shrink wrap material, standing on end, fell over and hit foot.	Bruised right big toe.	13	5
10.04	6 yrs 5 mths	A.L. Carvell Deepdale Dept.	F	37	Inspector	While opening cartons to inspect contents, she cut bend of small finger causing injury.	Very small cut to small finger of left hand.	2	1/14
03.04	2 yrs 8 mths	J.Y. Blincowe Plant and Services	M	62	Steel erector	While walking outside of Steel erector shop, he twisted his ankle.	Injury to right outer ankle.	9	14
23.03	1 yr	D.M. Hussein Receiving Stores	M	25	Labourer	While loading laundry onto trailer, he caught his knee on edge of trailer.	Pain in right knee.	16	4
07.04	8 yrs 3 mths	J. Austin Transport	M	48	Driver	While trailer was being parked at Deptford parking area, he was jammed between unit and wall.	Fractures to right collar bone, right arm and foot.	27	5
13.04	6 mths	G.I.K. Shemwell Transport	M	39	Fork lift driver	While loading pallets into trailer in Pressware Factory, he felt pain in his back.	Pain in lumbar region of back.	10	5

A safety committee may have noted that in less than a month:

- there was one **major injury** (involving both a fractured collar bone and a fractured arm) as defined under the RIDDOR Regulations (see Session B) and a potentially very serious accident (exploding flask);
- there were nine accidents involving absence from work of more than three days;
- several accidents involved lifting and handling operations;
- several relatively minor injuries resulted in several days off work;
- three new members of staff were involved in accidents;
- there was no 'near miss' data or data about accidents causing damage to property, equipment or stock; or accidents not causing lost time. This suggested that such incidents were not being reported.

Note that HSE must be notified whenever a person at work is incapacitated for normal work for more than three days as a result of an injury caused by an accident at work.

This short section should have given you an idea of the functions of safety representatives and safety committees.

You may also want to note the following point of law. Under the Trade Union Reform and Employment Rights Act 1993 and the Public Interest Disclosure Act 1999, all employees, regardless of their length of service, have a right to complain to an employment tribunal if they are dismissed or victimized for:

- carrying out any health and safety activities for which they have been designated by their employer;
- performing any functions as an official or employer-acknowledged health and safety representative or safety committee member;
- bringing a reasonable health and safety concern to their employer's attention in the absence of a representative or committee who could do so on their behalf;
- leaving their work area or taking other appropriate action in the face of serious and imminent danger.

Self-assessment 1

15 mins

1 Pick the correct statements from among the following.

a Statute law is derived from court decisions. ☐

b Contract law is relatively unimportant in health and safety matters. ☐

c Following an accident, an organization may be prosecuted under either criminal law or civil law. ☐

d European law takes precedence over UK law. ☐

e The Health and Safety at Work, etc. Act 1974 is a disabling Act. ☐

f The Health and Safety at Work, etc. Act 1974 places an obligation on employers to take care of the health and safety of customers on its premises. ☐

g Employees have duties to co-operate with employers in meeting the requirements of the law. ☐

h If an employee is given defective equipment, and gets hurt as a result, it's entirely the employer's fault. ☐

i 'As far as reasonably practicable' means that the degree of risk can be balanced against the cost of taking measures to avoid the risk. ☐

j 'So far as is practicable' means that the degree of risk can be balanced against the cost of taking measures to avoid the risk. ☐

2 The following statements about safety representatives have some words missing. Fill in the blanks from the words listed below.

Safety representatives may be involved in:

ACCIDENT   CO-OPERATION
HAZARDS   INSPECTIONS
PRACTICES   REPORTING
TALKING   UNSAFE
WELFARE   WORKPLACE

■ _____ to employees about particular health and safety problems;

■ encouraging _____ between their employer and employees;

■ carrying out _____ of the workplace to see whether there are any real or potential _____ that haven't been adequately addressed;

■ bringing to the attention of the employer any _____ or unhealthy conditions or working _____ , or unsatisfactory _____ arrangements;

■ _____ to employers about these problems and other matters connected to health and safety in that _____ ;

■ taking part in _____ investigations.

3 Match the correct description from the list on the right with each term on the left.

a	Approved codes of practice (ACOPs)	i	Acts of Parliament (such as the Health and Safety at Work, etc. Act 1974), together with a great many 'statutory instruments' or 'subordinate legislation'.
b	Civil law	ii	Stops, with immediate effect, people from carrying out activities that are considered to involve a risk of serious personal injury.
c	Prohibition notice	iii	Anyone committing a crime has offended against the state, and is in breach of this. If an organization fails to comply with its statutory health and safety duties, its officers may be prosecuted.
d	Criminal law	iv	A plaintiff sues a defendant, usually for damages, that is, financial compensation. As an example, an individual may sue an employer if he or she is injured at work.
e	EU Directives	v	Compels an employer to put right conditions that contravene the health and safety law.
f	Improvement notice	vi	Bind member countries to comply with an agreed ruling. They are normally made into national laws by each state.
i	Statute law	vii	Issued by the Health and Safety Commission (HSC) as interpretations of regulations, and are intended to help people apply the law in practice.

Answers to these questions can be found on pages 102–3.

7 Summary

- The law applicable in the UK is derived from three principal sources: statute law, common law, and contract law.

- Although it is important to distinguish between civil law and criminal law, both are important to organizations in terms of health and safety.

- Following an accident, actions may be brought against an organization through the criminal courts (for breach of statutory duty); through the civil courts (for breach of common law or statutory duty); or through an employment tribunal (for injury benefits).

- European laws take precedence over national laws in the courts, if ever there is any conflict.

- Approved Codes of Practice (ACOPs) are issued by the Health and Safety Commission (HSC) as interpretations of Regulations, and are intended to help people apply the law in practice. Guidance notes may include advice on action to be taken by employers in order to conform with the law.

- Both employers and employees have duties under the Health and Safety at Work, etc. Act 1974 (HSWA).

- The employer has a duty 'to ensure, as far as reasonably practicable, the health, safety and welfare at work of all his employees'. The employee has a duty to take reasonable care for the health and safety of himself and of other persons who may be affected by his acts or omissions at work.

- Every employer of five or more people must prepare and keep up to date a written statement of general policy with respect to the health and safety at work of employees, and the organization and arrangements for carrying out that policy, and to bring the statement and any revision of it to the notice of all employees.

- For all employers:

  - 'reasonably practicable' means that the degree of risk has to be balanced against the cost, time and difficulty of taking measures to avoid the risk;
  - 'practicable' means the cost, time and difficulty are not to be considered – technical feasibility is the only consideration;
  - 'absolute' – often indicated by the word 'shall' – means that the law must be obeyed.

- The Health and Safety Inspectorate have wide-reaching powers, including the right to enter and inspect any premises, at any time, where it is considered that there may be dangers to health or safety.

- A safety representative is someone appointed by a recognized trade union to represent employees on health and safety matters at work.

- An employer is legally obliged to set up a safety committee after receiving written requests to do so from two safety representatives.

Session B
Some important health and safety laws

1 Introduction

The Health and Safety at Work, etc. Act 1974 (HSWA) is a general enabling Act that allows Ministers to introduce more detailed Regulations and Approved Codes of Practice' (ACOPS) relating to health and safety without taking every single one through Parliament.

It is not a statutory requirement for organizations to follow each ACOP, **but** the Courts will regard following them as evidence that an organization is abiding by the 'letter and the spirit' of HSWA and subsequent Regulations. Any organization that ignores ACOPs, where they exist, does so at its peril.

1.1 Your liability under the law

It is a sound principle of English law that ignorance is no defence.
This makes perfect sense, for without it, the speeding motorist, the burglar and the murderer would all claim that they 'didn't know they were doing anything wrong'. This principle also applies to all Health and Safety law, and this can be a frightening thought.

In practice, you cannot possibly remember every aspect of every part of the law. What you **must** do is to check for your own specific job and team responsibilities which aspects of the law may apply. For example, if your team works with display screens, then, either directly or through your manager, you need to check how the Regulations and/or ACOP will apply to their work.

The principle that 'ignorance is no defence' is not as onerous to apply as it may sound. It simply requires you to check how the law affects what you are doing specifically; it **doesn't** demand that you know everything about Health and Safety Law – there are few people indeed who could claim that knowledge.

These Regulations are sometimes referred to as the 'six pack'. They comprise:

■ the Management of Health and Safety at Work Regulations 1999;
■ the Workplace (Health, Safety and Welfare) Regulations 1992;
■ the Manual Handling Operations Regulations 1992;
■ the Health and Safety (Display Screen Equipment) Regulations 1992;
■ the Personal Protective Equipment at Work Regulations 1992;
■ the Provision and Use of Work Equipment Regulations 1998.

Another very significant piece of legislation is the Control of Substances Hazardous to Health Regulations (COSHH) 1999.

In this session we will review all these Regulations, and, in addition, look briefly at a number of other Acts.

2 Management of Health and Safety at Work Regulations 1999 (MHSWR)

MHSWR applies to all kinds of work, apart from sea-going ships.

These regulations help to spell out the duties and responsibilities of employers much more explicitly than HSWA.

2.1 Main provisions of MHSWR

According to HSE:

'Their main provisions are designed to encourage a more systematic and better organized approach to dealing with health and safety.'

Specifically, MHSWR requires employers to:

1   undertake 'suitable and sufficient' assessments of risks to health and safety

MHSWR imposes a duty on employers to implement systematic risk assessments, which are recorded and updated whenever necessary.

The aim is to identify all significant risks in a workplace, to eliminate them wherever practicable and to minimize and control them where they cannot be eliminated.

Risk assessments must be recorded by all employers with more than five employees. They must be recorded in an accessible format, which may be paper-based or electronic.

In either case, the information must be accessible to HSE inspectors, safety representatives and other persons who have a right to gain access to the data.

2   implement necessary measures

Any required health and safety measures that follow from the risk assessment must then be put into practice.

EXTENSION 5
The approved code of practice, *Management of Health and Safety at Work Regulations, 1999* gives guidance on risk assessment.

Comment

To carry out a **risk assessment**, you must:

- identify the hazard;
- measure and evaluate the risk from this hazard;
- put measures into place that will either eliminate the hazard, or control it.

Example

In a work process involving the hand grinding of metal, one of the hazards is noise, and this fact must be recognized. During a risk assessment, the level of noise would need to be measured, and early action taken to protect workers – such as effective ear protectors.

For full coverage of risk assessment please refer to *Preventing Accidents* in this series.

3   provide health surveillance

Employers have to provide appropriate health surveillance for employees, where the risk assessment shows it to be necessary.

Comment

The purpose of **health surveillance** is to:

■ identify adverse affects early, well before disease becomes obvious;

■ rectify inadequacies in control, and so reduce the risks to those affected or exposed;

■ inform those at risk, as soon as possible, of any damage to their health, so that they can take action, and perhaps change their job;

■ to reinforce health education, for example, by reminding workers to use the personal protective equipment provided.

Those whose health should be closely monitored include people who:

■ work in dust-laden atmospheres;

■ handle toxic or harmful substances, such as lead, chromium or pesticides;

■ work in noisy environments;

■ use equipment or materials potentially damaging to the eyes.

---

4   appoint competent persons

The Regulations counsel employers to appoint 'competent persons' to provide the Health and Safety assistance referred to in the Regulations. The ACOP does not tell employers what a competent person is under all circumstances, or where such people may be found. For example:

■ large employers may have an Occupational Health and Safety section, staffed with suitably qualified people

■ smaller organizations may appoint a specific person who has adequate knowledge and experience of their operations, or they may buy in the required expertise from an external consultant who also has sufficient understanding of their operations.

Whatever action an organization takes to satisfy the need for competent persons, the responsibility for health, safety and welfare remains with the organization itself. Ultimately, in practice, this means the person who signs the Health and Safety Policy Statement.

Increasing attention is being focused on the responsibilities of company directors for health and safety, following disasters such as major rail crashes.

MHSWR emphasizes that organizations cannot absolve their senior management of ultimate responsibility, no matter how many advisors they may have.

5   provide information

Employees, together with temporary employees and others in the employer's organization, must be given information they can understand about health and safety matters.

2.1 Malicious assaults on staff and equipment

Unfortunately, cases of assault by members of the general public have become more common in some workplaces, including hospitals, schools, shops and places of entertainment. Many such problems are likely to occur at odd times, outside normal working hours.

In circumstances where such assaults may occur, the employer should deal with it as another risk to be assessed and eliminated or minimized. For example, by:

- installing practicable security measures to protect staff while at the same time allowing normal work to continue;
- training staff in techniques that help them recognize and, wherever possible, defuse uncontrolled anger that may lead to assaults;
- providing emergency measures, such as panic buttons and alarms linked to the local police station, for staff to use if matters are getting out of hand;
- ensuring that first aid facilities and trained first aiders are available whenever they may be required.

Malicious behaviour may also threaten equipment or stock. The measures implemented to minimise risk also need to protect items such as alcohol, fuel, drugs and explosives (fireworks), taking account of the degree of risk which they may pose.

Activity 13 ·

15 mins

S/NVQ A1.2

This Activity may provide the basis of appropriate evidence for your S/NVQ portfolio. If you are intending to take this course of action, it might be better to write your answers on separate sheets of paper.

As a team leader, you are expected to give information to your team members on their responsibilities for maintaining healthy, safe, and productive work conditions. This information should comply with your organization's requirements, and with the law.

Summarize the way that you currently go about fulfilling this responsibility.

_____

_____

_____

_____

_____

_____

Now write down the plans you have for improving the health and safety information you provide to your team.

_____

_____

_____

_____

_____

_____

Describe how you will ensure that they have understood this information.

_____

_____

_____

_____

_____

_____

To continue, MHSWR also requires employers to:

6 provide training

The Regulations impose detailed responsibilities for training, requiring employers to:

- assess the capabilities of employees relative to particular tasks, for instance in handling loads manually;
- provide induction training following recruitment;
- give training whenever their work changes in a way that may expose them to new or increased risks, when, for example, they are required to work on equipment or processes new to them, or with alterations to established systems of working;
- repeat training periodically as a refresher for established employees whenever necessary.

In effect, the regulations demand that employers carry out regular training needs analysis (TNA) and implement suitable training to meet the needs shown by the TNA.

Activity 14

3 mins

The law imposes a duty on employers to provide any necessary training on safe practices. Make a note of at least **three** aspects of safe practice in which you think the law would expect training and information to be provided.

For example: 'how to work safely in a particular job'.

_____

_____

_____

_____

_____

_____

Don't forget that, to your team you represent the employer.

An employee needs to know, through clear instructions and/or training, everything that concerns personal safety, including:

- how to work safely in his or her job;
- what to do if something goes wrong;

■ where to find safety equipment, and how to use it;
■ all relevant legal requirements;
■ what steps he or she needs to take to safeguard the safety of others;
■ any special hazards.

MHSWR also requires employers to:

7 set up emergency procedures

8 co-operate with any other employers who share a work site

9 place duties on employees to follow health and safety instructions and report danger

10 consult employees' safety representatives and provide facilities for them.

Consultation must now take place on such matters as the:

■ introduction of measures that may substantially affect health and safety;
■ arrangements for appointing competent persons;
■ health and safety information required by law;
■ health and safety aspects of new technology being introduced to the workplace.

To sum up

To repeat the main points included in MHSWR, employers must:

1 undertake 'suitable and sufficient' assessment of risks to health and safety;
2 implement necessary measures;
3 provide health surveillance;
4 appoint competent persons;
5 provide information;
6 provide training;
7 set up emergency procedures;
8 co-operate with any other employers who share a work site;
9 place duties on employees to follow health and safety instructions and report danger;
10 consult employees' safety representatives and provide facilities for them.

Activity 15

3 mins

Make a note of the aspects of MHSWR you think you are most likely to be involved in, in your job as first line manager.

_____

_____

_____

_____

_____

_____

Managers at all levels may be expected to participate in implementing MHSWR. In particular, you may have noted:

- implementing specific measures, following risk assessment;
- providing information and training for your team;
- helping to set up emergency procedures.

3 Workplace (Health, Safety and Welfare) Regulations 1992 (WHSWR)

These Regulations replace a total of 38 items of older legislation. They cover many aspects of health, safety and welfare in the workplace, and apply to most places of work.

They do **not** apply to:

- ships and boats;
- building operations or works of engineering construction;
- mines and mineral exploration sites;
- work on agricultural or forestry land away from main buildings.

WHSWR stipulates general requirements for working conditions, related to:

I   the working environment – including:

- ☐ temperature;
- ☐ ventilation;
- ☐ lighting;
- ☐ room dimensions;
- ☐ workstations and seating;
- ☐ outdoor workstations, such as weather protection.

Example

The Regulations say that:

'Effective and suitable provision shall be made to ensure that every enclosed workspace is ventilated by a sufficient quantity of fresh or purified air.'

In offices and many other workplaces, windows will provide enough ventilation. Alternatively, air conditioning systems may be installed.

Comment

Many of the requirements in these regulations appear to be 'common sense', and it is probably true to say that most workplaces are properly ventilated, heated and so on. Nevertheless, employers must obey the law.

---

2   safety – including:

- ☐ safe passage of pedestrians and vehicles;
- ☐ windows and skylights (safe opening, closing and cleaning);
- ☐ organization and control of traffic routes;
- ☐ glazed doors and partitions (use of safe material and marking);
- ☐ doors, gates and escalators (safety devices);
- ☐ floors (their construction and condition);
- ☐ obstructions and slipping and tripping hazards;
- ☐ falls from heights and into dangerous substances, and falling objects.

Example

The Regulations say that:

1 'Every workplace shall be organized in such a way that pedestrians and vehicles can circulate in a safe manner.
2 Traffic routes in a workplace shall be suitable for the persons or vehicles using them, sufficient in number, in suitable positions and of sufficient size.'

The Code of Practice reminds us that: 'In some situations, people in wheelchairs may be at greater risk than people on foot, and special consideration should be given to their safety.'

---

3 **welfare facilities** – including:

- [ ] toilets;
- [ ] washing, eating and changing facilities;
- [ ] provision of drinking water;
- [ ] clothing storage, and facilities for changing clothing;
- [ ] seating;
- [ ] rest areas (and arrangements in them for non-smokers);
- [ ] rest facilities for pregnant women and nursing mothers.

Example

The regulations say that:

'An adequate supply of drinking water shall be provided for all persons at work in the workplace.'

---

4 **housekeeping** – including:

- [ ] maintenance of workplace, equipment and facilities;
- [ ] cleanliness;
- [ ] removal of waste materials.

Activity 16 ·  3 mins

The Regulations are very detailed and complex. However you can make a note here if you want to find out more, and note the action you intend to take. (One way is to get hold of a copy of the Approved Code of Practice from the HSE, but you may be able to get the information through your organization. If you can get help with the interpretation of the Regulations, you should certainly do so.)

_____

_____

_____

_____

_____

_____

4 Manual Handling Operations Regulations 1992 (MHOR)

Accidents involving lifting and handling account for more than a third of all the accidents that cause people to be off work for more than three days, as reported through 'RIDDOR' (see page 57). That averages more than 45,000 accidents per year over a five-year period, not including the less serious ones which don't get into the published statistics.

EXTENSION 6
The Manual Handling
Operations Regulations
1992 are explained in
the HSE booklet _Manual
Handling – Guidance on
Regulations_.

The MHOR Regulations cover the lifting and manoeuvring of loads of all types. They require the employer to:

■ consider whether a load must be moved, and, if so, whether it could be moved by non-manual methods;

■ assess the risk in manual operations and (unless it is very simple) make a written record of this assessment;

■ reduce the risk of injury as far as is reasonably practicable.

The following is a summary of the questions that should be asked regarding four aspects of a manual handling operation.[1]

Making an assessment: some important questions

1 The task

- Is the load held or manipulated at a distance from the trunk, so increasing the stress on the lower back?

- Does the task involve:
    - twisting the trunk?
    - stooping?
    - reaching upwards?
    - excessive lifting or lowering distances?
    - excessive carrying distances?
    - pushing or pulling of the load?
    - a risk of sudden movement of the load?
    - frequent or prolonged physical effort?
    - insufficient rest or recovery periods?
    - a rate of work imposed by a process?

2 The load

- Is the load:
    - heavy?
    - bulky or unwieldy?
    - difficult to grasp?
    - unstable, or are its contents likely to shift?
    - sharp, hot or otherwise potentially damaging?

3 The working environment

- Are there:
    - space constraints preventing good posture?
    - uneven, slippery or unstable floors?
    - variations in the level of floors or work surfaces?
    - extremes of temperature or humidity?
    - ventilation problems or gusts of wind?
    - poor lighting conditions?

4 Individual capability

- Does the task require unusual strength, height, etc.?
- Does the job put at risk those who might be pregnant or have a health problem?
- Does the task require special information or training for its safe performance?

[1] Adapted from *Manual Handling – Guidance on Regulations* published by HSE, pages 12–20.

Activity 17 · 3 mins

	Yes	No
Does your team's job involve manual handling?	☐	☐
Are you confident that you are managing manual handling tasks efficiently and effectively?	☐	☐

If not, how will you learn more?

_____

_____

_____

Almost **every** job involves manual handling at some stage, and you don't have to be lifting heavy weights to become injured if you do it wrongly . It is for these reasons that the MHOR are so important to all managers, from legal, commercial and moral perspectives.

5 Health and Safety (Display Screen Equipment) Regulations 1992

EXTENSION 7
VDUs: an easy guide to the Regulations. How to comply with the Health and Safety (display screen equipment) Regulations 1992.

These Regulations put into law the employer's duties regarding the operation of display screen equipment by employees. Employers have to:

■ assess and reduce the risks from display screen equipment;
■ make sure that workstations satisfy minimum requirements;
■ plan to allow breaks or change of activity;
■ provide information and training for users;
■ give users eye and eyesight tests and (if need be) special glasses.

Display screen equipment includes cathode ray tubes (CRTs), liquid crystal displays, and any other technology.

The Regulations do not apply to:

- drivers' cabs or control cabs for vehicles and machinery;
- display screen equipment on board a means of transport;
- display screen equipment mainly intended for public operation;
- portable systems not in prolonged use;
- calculators, cash registers or any equipment having a small data or measurement display required for direct use of the equipment;
- window typewriters.

The figure, and the text below it, summarize the minimum requirements for workstations.[2]

Key to illustration:

1	Adequate lighting	7	Screen: stable image, adjustable, readable, glare/reflection free
2	Adequate contrast, no glare or distracting reflections		
		8	Keyboard: usable, adjustable, detachable, legible
3	Distracting noise minimized		
4	Leg room and clearances to allow postural changes	9	Work surface: allow flexible arrangements, spacious, glare free
5	Window covering		
6	Software: appropriate to task, adapted to user, provides feedback on system status, no undisclosed monitoring	10	Work chair: adjustable
		11	Footrest

2 Figure and text from *Display Screen Equipment Work – Guidance on Regulations* published by HSE.

Activity 18 · 3 mins

	Yes	No
Does your team's job involve working with display screen equipment for long periods?	☐	☐
Are you confident that you comply with the law?	☐	☐

If not, how will you learn more?

_____

_____

_____

_____

_____

6 Personal Protective Equipment at Work Regulations 1992 (PPEWR)

Personal protective equipment (PPE) includes eye, foot and head protection equipment, safety harnesses, life jackets, and so on. Employers have to:

■ ensure that this equipment is suitable and appropriate;
■ maintain, clean and replace it;
■ provide storage for it when not in use;
■ ensure that it is properly used;
■ give employees training, information and instruction in its use.

It is illegal for an employer who provides PPE to make any charge to someone using it.

Complete the following Activity, to help you decide what further action you need to take regarding PPE.

Activity 19

10 mins

S/NVQ A1.2

If your team needs to use personal protective equipment, or you think they may need to use it, answer the questions below.

- Is the equipment appropriate to the risks, and to the conditions at the place where exposure might occur? ☐

- Does it take account of ergonomic requirements, and the state of health of the persons who may wear it? ☐

- Does it fit the wearer? ☐

- Is it effective in preventing or controlling the risk? ☐

- Is it compatible with other equipment? ☐

- Have all the following risks been assessed?

Head injury?	☐	Eye injury?	☐
Face injury?	☐	Inhalation of airborne contaminants?	☐
Noise-induced hearing loss?	☐	Skin contact?	☐
Bodily injury?	☐	Hand or arm injury?	☐
Leg or foot injury?	☐	Vibration-induced injury?	☐

- Is appropriate accommodation provided for the PPE when it isn't in use? ☐

- Have the users been given adequate information, instruction and training? ☐

- Do all the users:

  - use the equipment in accordance with their training and instructions? ☐

  - return the PPE to its accommodation after use? ☐

  - understand the need to report losses or defects? ☐

What further actions do you intend to take about PPE?

_____

_____

_____

_____

_____

7 Provision and Use of Work Equipment Regulations 1998 (PUWER)

The definition of 'work equipment' is very wide, and includes a butcher's knife, a combine harvester and even a complete power station. Employers must:

- take into account working conditions and hazards when selecting equipment;
- ensure equipment is suitable for use, and is properly maintained;
- provide adequate instruction, information and training.

The next Activity is a very brief summary checklist. Complete it to help you decide what action you might want to take in regard to work equipment.

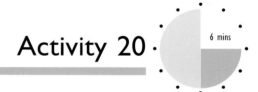

Activity 20

6 mins

Portfolio of evidence

S/NVQ A1.2

Identify an important item of equipment that your team works with. Then answer the following questions about it.

Item: _____

- Is the equipment suitable for the use it is put to? ☐
- Is it well and regularly maintained? ☐
- Are adequate information and instructions available to potential users? ☐
- Have the users received adequate training in its use? ☐
- Have you provided protection against dangerous parts of the equipment, such as guards around rotating parts? ☐
- Have measures been taken to eliminate or control risks associated with the use of the equipment? ☐
- Are stop controls provided that are easy to reach, and well marked? ☐

- Are control systems (if any) safe? ☐
- Is isolation provided from sources of energy? ☐
- Is the equipment stable? ☐
- Is it well lit, and marked with appropriate signs and warnings? ☐

Do you need to find out more about the use of work equipment, or these Regulations? Write down any actions you intend to take.

_____

_____

_____

_____

_____

_____

So much for the six Regulations that form the 'six pack'. Now we will look at another very important set of Regulations.

8 Control of Substances Hazardous to Health Regulations 1994 (COSHH)

COSHH doesn't cover asbestos, lead, materials producing ionizing radiation and substances below ground in mines, which all have their own legislation.

The Control of Substances Hazardous to Health Regulations (COSHH) potentially affect any substance used for any purpose in the workplace. Even food ingredients can be hazardous in some circumstances. Sugar can be involved in dust explosions and flour can be implicated in occupational asthma.

The Regulations require users to carry out risk assessments on every **potentially** hazardous substance and to take appropriate action when the assessment has been made.

Activity 21

3 mins

Can you think of any substances which could possibly affect the health of people where you work?

_____

_____

_____

_____

_____

_____

_____

There are over 40,000 substances which are classed as hazardous. Wherever you work – in a food factory, a shop, a garage, a warehouse, a laboratory, an engineering works, a hospital, a farm, a garden centre or an office – hazardous substances will probably be present. They may include:

- anything brought into a workplace to be worked on, used or stored, including corrosives, acids or solvents used in cleaning materials;
- dust and fumes given off by a work process;
- finished products or residues from a work process.

Example of label

Toxic or very toxic

Anything very toxic, toxic, corrosive, harmful or irritant comes under COSHH. Examples are chemicals, agricultural pesticides, wood treatment chemicals, dusts and substances containing harmful micro-organisms. By law, the containers of hazardous substances must be labelled as being hazardous, and they must state what the hazard is.

Assessing the hazards of substances and the potential harm if they are mixed with **other** substances is a highly technical subject. The law recognizes this and requires specialist manufacturers and suppliers of substances to provide comprehensive information to users (usually in the form of data sheets) to help guard them against risks which they may not have the technical knowledge to anticipate. Manufacturers will also provide further data on request as a part of their obligations under COSHH.

Activity 22 · 15 mins

EXTENSION 8 is a model data sheet which might be used by the manufacturer of a chemical product.

Find an example of a data sheet relating to a hazardous substance in your own department or organisation. Then make sure that you know where the data sheets are kept for all hazardous substances with which you might come into contact.

8.1 Employers' duties under COSHH

Under the COSHH Regulations, employers have to:

Example of label

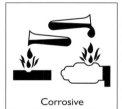

Corrosive

- **determine the hazard** of substances used by the organization;
- **assess the risk** to people's health from the way the substances are used;
- **prevent anyone being exposed** to the substances, if possible;
- if exposure cannot be prevented, decide how to **control the exposure** so as to **reduce the risk**, and then establish effective controls;
- ensure that the controls are **properly used and maintained**;
- **examine and test the control measures**, if this is required;
- **inform, instruct and train** employees (and non-employees on the premises), so that they are aware of the hazards and how to work safely;
- if necessary, **monitor the exposure** of employees (and non-employees on the premises), and provide **health surveillance** to employees if necessary.

8.2 Your job and COSHH

Now let us consider what impact COSHH has on your job.

Activity 23 · 5 mins

From what you've read so far, can you suggest how first line managers and team leaders can play a part in helping their employer comply with the COSHH Regulations, and so reduce the risk to employees from hazardous substances? Try to list **two** or **three** positive actions that might be taken by someone in your position.

_____

_____

_____

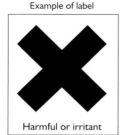

Example of label

Harmful or irritant

■ Probably the most important role first-line managers and team leaders can play is in informing and training the workteam about the hazards and the correct procedures to be followed. We'll look at the kind of information and training needed in a moment.

■ They can and should ensure that safety procedures are followed, and set a personal example in following the correct procedures consistently and carefully.

■ Team leaders are also usually in a good position to assess the likely behaviour of people when they have to deal with hazardous situations. If so, they can assist their employer in determining what people do and what they might do.

■ If protective clothing and/or emergency facilities are provided, it is often the team leader's job to ensure that these items are available when they're needed, and are properly maintained.

■ Leaders should ensure that the only substances used are those whose risks have been assessed, and that team members have been trained in the safe handling of these substances.

Let's now look at the aspects of training and providing information to staff about hazardous substances.

A team leader will need to make sure of the following.

■ **Team members should understand the hazards.**

All suppliers are compelled by law to label hazardous substances. Everyone using such a substance needs to be trained to read and understand container labels and to follow the supplier's advice.

■ **Team members should understand how risks are controlled.**

Procedures for controlling risks must be clearly laid down.

■ **Team members should understand the precautions they have to take.**

Precautions and procedures will almost certainly need to be demonstrated.

■ **Team members should understand what to do in the case of an emergency.**

Emergency procedures need to be demonstrated and practised.

■ **Team members should always feel able to ask for guidance.**

There should be an atmosphere of trust so that if people are not sure of the right course of action in particular circumstances, they feel free to ask for help or advice from their manager, specialist advisors, or the manufacturer.

Activity 24 · 6 mins

S/NVQ A1.2

This Activity may provide the basis of appropriate evidence for your S/NVQ portfolio. If you are intending to take this course of action, it might be better to write your answers on separate sheets of paper.

There are few workplaces where hazardous substances do not exist. If you have hazardous substances in your work area, what training does your team receive about them? Summarize the kind of training they get.

_____

_____

_____

_____

_____

_____

Based on the points listed above, write down your plans for improving their training in this important area.

_____

_____

_____

_____

_____

_____

_____

What further actions do you think you need to take, in order to comply with COSHH? (You may decide to find out more about the Regulations before you answer this.)

_____

_____

_____

_____

_____

_____

Now we have covered the 'six-pack' Regulations, and looked at COSHH, we move on to some other important health and safety laws.

9 Other laws

HSWA and the Regulations and ACOPs discussed earlier in this session deal with the greater proportion of general health, safety and welfare at work issues. They replace the former piecemeal approach with a general preventive approach.

However, the vast library of legislation in this field includes many earlier laws which remain on the statute book. Many of these are Regulations specific to activities of particular industries, such as electricity.

Specific legislation still in force includes:

■ Factories Act, 1961;
■ Offices, Shops and Railway Premises Act, 1963;
■ Health and Safety (Young Persons) Regulations 1999;
■ Electricity at Work Regulations, 1989;
■ Health and Safety (First Aid) Regulations, 1981;
■ Noise at Work Regulations, 1989;
■ Reporting of Injuries, Diseases and Dangerous Occurrences Regulations, 1995;
■ Public Interest Disclosure Act 1999 (PIDA).

9.1 Factories Act 1961 and Offices, Shops and Railway Premises Act 1963

Most of the provisions of these two Acts have been replaced by subsequent Regulations such as the Workplace (Health, Safety and Welfare) Regulations 1992 (WHSWR), the Provision and Use of Work Equipment Regulations 1998 (PUWER) and the Health and Safety (Young Persons) Regulations 1999.

This subsection discusses some of the Regulations which may affect you directly or indirectly, for example, where contractors are working in or near your team location.

9.2 Health and Safety (Young Persons) Regulations 1999

Accident statistics show that young people (anyone under 18) are especially vulnerable to accidents at work. These Regulations prohibit them from operating or cleaning some prescribed dangerous machines, and set out additional requirements as to their training and supervision.

If your team includes young people, talk to your manager if you have any doubts as to what you should do to ensure their safety.

Further guidance is available from the HSE publication HSG165 Young people at Work – a Guide for Employers.

9.3 Electricity at Work Regulations 1989

The purpose of these Regulations is to require that precautions be taken to prevent the risk of death or injury from electricity at work. They set out general principles for electrical safety, rather than specifying detailed requirements.

Subjects covered include:

- earthing or other suitable precautions;
- the means of protecting from excess current;
- the means of cutting off the supply and of isolation;
- people's competence to prevent danger or injury.

9.4 Health and Safety (First Aid) Regulations, 1981

Under this regulation, all employers in the UK are required to do the following.

- Provide first aid.

  Equipment and facilities must be provided that are 'adequate and appropriate' in the circumstances for enabling first aid to be rendered to employees if they are injured or become ill at work.

- Inform employees of first aid arrangements.

9.5 Noise at Work Regulations 1989

Noise causes hearing damage, and the damage is accumulative: the longer you are exposed to excessive levels of noise, the more likely you are to suffer hearing loss.

Noise is measured in Decibels (dB) on a logarithmic scale, which makes for some perhaps surprising readings. For example:

- when the measure increases from 87dB to 90dB, the noise is actually **doubling**
- if the noise level needs to be reduced from 90dB to 87dB, then the requirement is to **halve** it. This may be difficult and expensive to do.

The Regulations 'are intended to reduce hearing damage caused by loud noise'. They specify three action levels:

- at the 'first action level' (measured as 85dB(A)), employers must:
  - get noise assessed by a competent person, and keep a record;
  - inform employees about the risks to their hearing;
  - provide ear protectors if requested;
  - advise any employees who think their hearing is being affected to seek medical advice.

As a rough check, at this noise level it begins to be difficult to hear what someone is saying when they are two metres away.

- at the second and peak action levels (measured as 90dB(A) and 140dB respectively), the noise exposure must be controlled, preferably by reducing the noise and, as a last resort, by providing ear protectors.

The diagram shows typical noise levels associated with work activities. The bands show the length of time that workers can be exposed to such noise before their 'noise dose' exceeds the action levels.

Redrawn from *Essentials of Health and Safety at Work*, published by HSE. Reproduced with kind permission of HMSO.[3]

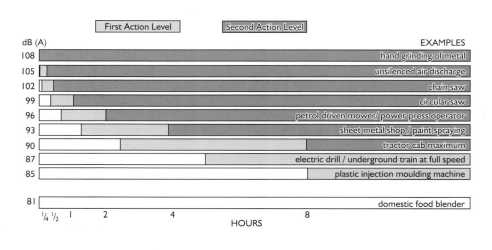

[3] Crown copyright 1990

Activity 25 ·

2 mins

According to the above diagram, approximately how much time should be allowed to lapse before someone exposed to the noise of a chain saw:

a   is informed about the risks to their hearing: _____

b   is provided with ear protectors: _____

The best answer, in both cases, is 'no time at all'. According to the diagram, a chain saw is likely to be around 102dB(A). This is above the first action level of 85dB(A), so a known risk exists, and after only a very short time the 'noise dose' will have exceeded that advisable at this level. After around half an hour, the second action level is invoked. Having this information, anyone working with a chain saw should know to wear ear protectors all the time.

You don't have to be working with power tools to be in a noisy environment. Many places of entertainment generate noise levels well above the first action level, as do bottling plants and warehouses where metal racks are being constantly moved around.

9.6   Reporting of Injuries, Diseases and Dangerous Occurrences Regulations 1995 (RIDDOR)

Whenever any of the following events occurs, RIDDOR states that it must be reported in writing to the enforcing authority (usually the HSE). In addition, an event of type 1, 2 or 3 must first of all be notified to the enforcing authority 'by quickest practicable means'.[4]

1   the **death** of any person as a result of an accident arising out of or in connection with work;

---

[4] This section (from 'Whenever any of the following events occurs' to 'but not more than one year afterwards') adapted from HSE Booklet HSE 11 (Rev) 5/86 © Crown copyright

2 any person at work suffering any of **certain injuries** or conditions as a result of an accident arising out of or in connection with work, including:

- **fracture of the skull, spine or pelvis;**
- **fracture of any bone** except in the hand or foot;
- **amputation** of: a hand or foot; or a finger, thumb or toe;
- **loss of the sight** of an eye or serious injury to the eye;
- injury as a result of **electric shock;**
- **loss of consciousness resulting from lack of oxygen;**
- acute illness requiring medical treatment, or loss of consciousness, resulting from **absorption of any substance by inhalation, ingestion or through the skin;**
- acute illness requiring medical treatment resulting from **exposure to a pathogen** (such as a bacterium or virus) **or infected material;**
- any other **injury that results in the person injured being admitted immediately into hospital for more than twenty-four hours**.

3 any **dangerous occurrence**, such as an overturned crane or burst pressure vessel;

4 an employee or other person at work **being incapacitated for normal work for more than three days** as a result of an injury caused by an accident at work;

5 the **death of an employee** if this occurs some time after the reportable injury that led to the employee's death, but not more than one year afterwards.

The relevant HSE forms are F2508 (Report of an injury or dangerous occurrence) and F2508A (Report of a case of a disease).

You may find it helpful to distinguish between the aims of RIDDOR and MHSWR.

Reports under RIDDOR are made **after** a serious incident has occurred.

The essence of MHSWR is that employers should anticipate risks to health and safety and act **before** they happen to eliminate or mitigate them.

Under MHSWR, employers are required to anticipate 'serious and imminent dangers' and

- establish procedures to be followed should such a circumstance arise;
- nominate competent persons (that is people with sufficient training and experience) to deal with the particular events anticipated;
- ensure that no-one enters a designated danger area (for example, a vessel or area containing toxic gas) without adequate training.

9.7 Public Interest Disclosure Act 1999 (PIDA)

This Act protects workers at any level from being penalized by their employer for bringing safety failures to public attention. It is often referred to as the 'whistle blowing' Act.

Under PIDA it is automatically unfair to dismiss an employee for raising genuine safety concerns either within the organization or directly with a 'prescribed regulator'. The HSE is one of a list of more than 30 prescribed regulators with whom an employee can raise concerns directly.

A number of cases have gone to employment tribunals under this legislation. Substantial awards have been made for unfair dismissal and factors such as hurt feelings.

9.8 Industry-specific legislation and help

HSE Publications are available from their website: www.hsebooks.co.uk

The health and safety laws we have looked at are applicable to most places of work. Other regulations are aimed specifically at certain industry sectors, and you will need to follow up any that are relevant to your area of work. Some examples are:

- Dangerous Substances in Harbour Area Regulations 1987;
- Docks Regulations 1988;
- Loading and Unloading of Fishing Vessels Regulations 1998;
- Escape and Rescue from Mines Regulations 1993;
- Offshore Installations and Pipeline Works (First Aid) Regulations 1989;
- Quarries Regulations, 1999;
- Carriage of Dangerous Goods by Road Regulations 1996.

HSE also gives specific guidance on the way that general legislation applies to specific industries.

Self-assessment 2

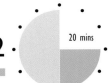

20 mins

1   Match each requirement under the Management of Health and Safety at Work Regulations, (MHSWR) on the left with the correct comment on the right.

Under MHSWR, employers must: **This includes the process of:**

a   provide risk assessment

i   identifying adverse affects; rectifying inadequacies in control; informing those at risk of any damage to their health; reinforcing health education

b   provide health surveillance

ii   identifying measures that may substantially affect health and safety; identifying health and safety aspects of new technology; discussing these with the relevant people

c   appoint competent persons

iii   identifying the hazard; measuring and evaluating the risk from this hazard; putting measures into place that will either eliminate the hazard, or control it

d   consult employees' safety representatives

iv   identifying those with sufficient training, and experience or knowledge and other qualities; requiring them to devise and apply the measures needed to comply with health and safety laws.

2   For each activity on the left, identify **one** regulation that will apply to it, taken from the list on the right.

Activity

i   Loading bags of flour

_____

ii   Supervising telesales

_____

iii   Running an electrical department in a superstore

_____

iv   Training fork-lift truck drivers in a fuel depot

_____

v   Supervising an area where there are high levels of dust

_____

vi   Supervising on a building site

_____

Regulation

a   Management of Health and Safety at Work Regulations (MHSWR)

b   Workplace (Health, Safety and Welfare) Regulations (WHSWR)

c   Manual Handling Operations Regulations (MHOR)

d   Health and Safety (Display Screen Equipment) Regulations

e   Personal Protective Equipment at Work (PPE) Regulations (PPEWR)

3 Fill in the blanks in the following statements with suitable words taken from the list below.

CONTROL   INSTRUCT   SAFELY
CONTROLS   MAINTAINED   SUBSTANCES
EXPOSED   MONITOR   SURVEILLANCE
HAZARD   RISK   TEST
HEALTH

Under the COSHH Regulations, employers have to:

■ determine the _____ of _____ used by the organization;

■ assess the _____ to people's health from the way the substances are used;

■ prevent anyone being _____ to the substances, if possible;

■ if exposure cannot be prevented, decide how to _____ the exposure so as to reduce the risk, and then establish effective _____ ;

■ ensure that the controls are properly used and _____ ;

■ examine and _____ the control measures, if this is required;

■ inform, _____ and train employees (and non-employees on the premises), so that they are aware of the hazards and how to work _____;

■ if necessary, _____ the exposure of employees (and non-employees on the premises), and provide _____ _____ to employees if necessary.

Answers to these questions can be found on pages 103–4.

10 Summary

■ The Management of Health and Safety at Work Regulations 1999 (MHSWR) are designed to encourage a more systematic and better organized approach to dealing with health and safety.

■ Under MHSWR, employers must:

  ■ assess the risks of the job;
  ■ implement necessary measures;
  ■ provide health surveillance;
  ■ appoint competent persons;
  ■ provide information and training;
  ■ set up emergency procedures;
  ■ co-operate with any other employers who share a work site;
  ■ place duties on employees to follow health and safety instructions and report danger;
  ■ consult employees' safety representatives and provide facilities for them.

■ The Workplace (Health, Safety and Welfare) Regulations 1992 (WHSWR) stipulates general requirements for working conditions, related to:

  ■ the working environment;
  ■ safety;
  ■ welfare facilities;
  ■ housekeeping.

■ The Manual Handling Operations Regulations 1992 (MHOR) require the employer to:

  ■ consider whether a load must be moved, and if so, whether it could be moved by non-manual methods;
  ■ assess the risk in manual operations and (unless it is very simple) make a written record of this assessment;
  ■ reduce the risk of injury as far as is reasonably practicable.

■ The Health and Safety (Display Screen Equipment) Regulations 1992 require employers to:

  ■ assess and reduce the risks from display screen equipment;
  ■ make sure that workstations satisfy minimum requirements;
  ■ plan to allow breaks or change of activity;
  ■ provide information and training for users;
  ■ give users eye and eyesight tests and (if need be) special glasses.

■ The Personal Protective Equipment at Work (PPE) Regulations 1992 (PPEWR) require employers to:

  ■ ensure PPE equipment is suitable and appropriate;
  ■ maintain, clean and replace it;
  ■ provide storage for it when not in use;
  ■ ensure that it is properly used;
  ■ give employees training, information and instruction in its use.

- The Provision and Use of Work Equipment Regulations 1998 (PUWER) require employers to:

  - take into account working conditions and hazards when selecting equipment;
  - ensure equipment is suitable for use, and is properly maintained;
  - provide adequate instruction, information and training.

- Under the Control of Substances Hazardous to Health Regulations, 1999 (COSHH) regulations, employers have to:

  - determine the hazard of substances used by the organization;
  - assess the risk to people's health from the way the substances are used;
  - prevent anyone being exposed to the substances, if possible;
  - if exposure cannot be prevented, decide how to control the exposure so as to reduce the risk, and then establish effective controls;
  - ensure that the controls are properly used and maintained;
  - examine and test the control measures, if this is required;
  - inform, instruct and train employees (and non-employees on the premises), so that they are aware of the hazards and how to work safely;
  - if necessary, monitor the exposure of employees (and non-employees on the premises), and provide health surveillance to employees if necessary.

- Other laws we looked at were:

  - the Factories Act 1961;
  - the Offices, Shops and Railway Premises Act 1963;
  - the Health and Safety (Young Persons) Regulations 1999
  - the Electricity at Work Regulations 1989;
  - the Health and Safety (First Aid) Regulations 1981;
  - the Noise at Work Regulations 1989;
  - the Reporting of Injuries, Diseases and Dangerous Occurrences Regulations 1995;
  - the Public Interest Disclosure Act 1999.

Session C
The law on the environment

1 Introduction

What do we mean by the environment? Albert Einstein is said to have defined it as 'everything that isn't me'. The law is a little more specific: the Environmental Protection Act, 1990 expressed it as 'all, or any, of the following media, namely air, water and land'.

1.1 The environment under threat

Many business activities have the potential to pollute one or more aspects of the environment. You don't have to run a steelworks or chemical plant to cause significant pollution. For example:

- burning rubbish as a standard way of disposing of it pollutes the atmosphere;
- tipping waste chemicals or frying oil into the drains will pollute water supplies;
- 'fly tipping' of building rubble will pollute the land, especially if the waste contains hazardous substances such as asbestos.

It is not only pollution that threatens our environment in the future. The activities of humans have increased the amounts of carbon gases collecting in the atmosphere, so tending to upset the natural balance between the short-wavelength ultra-violet radiation energy from the sun absorbed by the earth and the re-radiation of long-wavelength infra-red radiation. This could have devastating effects throughout the world, including:

- raising the temperature on the surface of the earth;
- melting glaciers and ice-caps;
- raising sea levels;
- flooding large areas of land;
- ruining crops through drought.

1.2 The need for control

In practice threats to the environment do not come from a few large sources; they are the sum of millions of actions each year by countless businesses and individuals.

Environmental laws are necessary, but they are not the only reason for managing a business to minimize pollution and waste.

As with health and safety at work, there are moral and commercial reasons for minimizing waste and the pollution associated with it. Some of these are:

- an inefficient boiler plant wastes costly fuel;
- over-use of fertilizers is inefficient and costly;
- sending excessive amounts of packaging or off cuts to the dump wastes valuable raw materials.

An environmentally friendly plant is also an efficient one. Increasing numbers of organizations recognize this and are adopting **environmental policies** to meet their commercial needs, as well as their moral and legal obligations. These policies are equivalent to the Health and Safety Policy Statement required under HSWA. Help in developing them is available from British Standards, for example, through their BS14001 environmental management system, equivalent to the BS9000 series for quality, and from 'Envirowise' a government programme offering free, independent advice on practical ways to minimise waste and convert turnover into profit.

Poor production practices not only pollute the environment and increase global warming, but also accelerate the rate at which scarce natural resources are used up. Some of the resources most at risk are:

- oil, natural gas and coal;
- mineral ores and deposits;
- water. It has recently been estimated that 50% of the world's population will be suffering from water shortages by 2030.

2 Background to environmental law

Though British legislation on pollution goes back to the Middle Ages, the first significant law dates from the Industrial Revolution. This was the Public Health Act 1875.

Another notable landmark was the formation of the Alkali Inspectorate in 1863 in order to control emissions into the atmosphere caused by the caustic soda industry. It was in fact the world's first national pollution control agency. However, in the past most public health and environmental protection was carried out locally rather than nationally.

Also, until fairly recently, laws tended to be passed in response to particular problems rather than being planned so as to take care of the environment as a whole: they were reactive, rather than proactive. An example of this was the Deposit of Poisonous Wastes Act 1972, which was a reaction to the much-reported fly-tipping of poisonous waste near a school playground, and which was approved by Parliament in only a few days.

2.1 Sources of environmental law

Unlike health and safety, very little case law has any relevance to environmental law, which is virtually all statutory.

The Health and Safety at Work, etc. Act 1974 (HSWA) has a number of provisions dealing with the environment, as is indicated by the full title of Part I of the Act:

> 'Health, Safety and Welfare in connection with Work and Control of Dangerous Substances and Certain Emissions into the Atmosphere'.

However, environmental law typically consists of framework Acts which give rise to Regulations that spell out the detail. An example is the Environmental Protection Act 1990, which made it compulsory for authorization to be obtained before 'prescribed processes' could be carried on by industry. The actual processes were not mentioned in the Act, but were listed in the Environmental Protection (Prescribed Processes and Substances) Regulations 1991.

The COSHH Regulations, whose impact on health and safety was examined in some depth in Session B, also affect management from the environmental point of view.

In particular, the Regulations require users to assess the risks from:

■ fumes;
■ by-products or decomposition products;
■ routine disposal methods;
■ leaks and spillages.

Activity 26 · 5 mins

Take one product used either directly by your team or elsewhere in your workplace, and make a note of the procedures to be followed in respect of:

■ routine disposal procedure;
■ dealing with spillages.

Disposal procedure

_____

_____

_____

Spillage procedure

_____

_____

_____

The transport of dangerous substances is a particular area to be concerned about. Accidents involving the transport of dangerous substances by road, rail, sea, air and pipeline are rare, but can have devastating local to global environmental effects. The HSE publishes many guidance notes for organizations involved with such transportation.

If your work is involved with these areas, check what information is available through your employer and/or is listed in the HSE Books Catalogue, available free from HSE Books.

Activity 27 · 2 mins

Statute law is passed by the members of the Houses of Parliament. What body outside this country would you expect to have a considerable influence on environmental law?

_____

_____

Thinking back to the sources of health and safety law, you might have reasoned that the European Union would be of enormous importance in the environmental field.

As in other fields, EU environmental law is normally introduced to member countries by means of Directives, which require national laws to be passed to bring them into line with EU law. For example, the Wildlife and Countryside Act, 1981 was introduced so as to comply with an EU Directive on wild birds; at the same time, the opportunity was taken to change a number of other areas of the law.

Some further examples of subjects on which EU Directives have been issued include:

- quality standards for water;
- quality standards for air;
- noise standards;
- lead in petrol;
- the storage and use of hazardous materials;
- the disposal of freezers and refrigerators.

The environmental policies of the EU have already greatly influenced British environmental legislation, and are likely to continue to do so in the future. The basic principles of these policies are that:

- **preventative action is to be preferred** to remedial measures;
- environmental **damage should be rectified at source**;
- **the polluter should pay** for the costs of the measures taken to protect the environment;
- environmental policies should form a component of the EU's other policies.

The first point of policy – that preventative action is to be preferred to remedial measures – contrasts with the traditional approach, in which governments tended to react to problems rather than trying to prevent them.

The 'polluter pays' principle is also a change to previous practice. What it means is that producers of goods or services should be responsible for the costs of preventing or dealing with any pollution that they may cause. This includes both direct costs in the form of recompense to people and repairs to property, and environmental costs.

This does **not** mean that it is acceptable for organizations to pollute the environment, provided they pay for clearing up the mess afterwards.

What about outside Europe?

Activity 28

5 mins

The governments and people of many countries believe that other states should not be allowed to interfere in their activities. The main protagonists for this argument include the United States (the world's largest generator of pollution) and developing countries such as India, Indonesia and China.

What do you think about this? Do you believe it is a realistic attitude towards pollution and one that UK citizens would be right to share?

_____

_____

_____

The environment has no national boundaries, and pollution cannot always be contained within one country. We were reminded of this fact in a rather grim fashion following the Chernobyl disaster in 1986.

Chernobyl is 130 km north of Kiev, in central Ukraine. On 26 April 1986, a nuclear power plant there went out of control and caused the worst reactor disaster the world has known to date. During a period of maintenance, an experiment was conducted with the water-cooling system turned off, which led to an uncontrolled reaction. The subsequent explosion of steam blew off the reactor's protective covering, releasing around 100 million curies of radionuclides into the atmosphere. The radiation spread across northern Europe and some of it settled in the UK, contaminating large areas of land.

All countries need to co-operate on environmental matters; international law, which governs relations between countries, also influences UK environmental law. For example, the North Sea Conferences had a substantial impact on the law related to the dumping of sewage sludge in the North Sea.

2.2 Areas of environmental law

There are four principal areas of environmental law:

■ pollution;
■ water;
■ nature conservation;
■ town and country planning.

3 Principal environmental legislation

The Environmental Protection Act 1990 (EPA) brought in some fundamental changes with regard to the control of pollution and the protection of the environment.

3.1 The Environmental Protection Act 1990

Specifically, this Act covers:

■ **air pollution** (but not vehicle emissions);
■ **waste management and disposal**;
■ **integrated pollution control (IPC)**; (we will discuss integrated pollution control shortly);
■ litter;
■ the environmental impact of genetically modified organisms;
■ noise;
■ statutory control of environmental nuisances.

3.2 The Environment Act 1995

> 'Contaminated land' is any land which appears to be in such a condition that significant harm, or pollution of inland or coastal waters, is caused, or is likely to be caused.

The Environment Act 1995 created the **Environment Agency** for England and Wales. This body came into being on 1 April 1996, taking over the powers of HM Inspectorate of Pollution, the National Rivers Authority, and local waste regulation authorities. In Scotland, the equivalent body is the Scottish Environment Protection Agency, and in N. Ireland it is the Environment and Heritage Service.

The Environment Act also:

- established a national **strategy and framework for air quality** standards, and targets for nine types of pollutant;
- gave new powers to local authorities to **review air quality** in their areas;
- reinforced the '**polluter pays**' policy in respect of **contaminated land**, but recognized that land-owners should also take responsibility for some aspects;
- made **sustainable development** a cornerstone of national waste strategies, which means making the best possible use of unavoidable waste, and minimizing the risk of pollution or harm to health arising from waste disposal or recovery;
- introduced regulations to impose **producer responsibility** to increase the re-use, recovery or recycling of any product or material;
- made water companies responsible for the **efficient use of water** by their customers;
- gave the Environmental Agency powers to require action to **prevent water pollution**, and to require polluters to clean up after pollution incidents.

3.3 Other environmental legislation

Most of the legislation on water pollution is now contained in the Water Resources Act 1991.

The Wildlife and Countryside Act 1981 includes much of the law on nature conservation.

The Town and Country Planning Act 1990 contains most of the law on town and country planning and tree protection.

We will look into some of these Acts in more detail later in this Session.

In addition to these main Acts on environmental law, there is separate legislation to cover other kinds of pollution, including vehicle emissions and pesticides.

4 Integrated pollution control

The concept of **integrated pollution control (IPC)** was introduced by the Environmental Protection Act 1990.

4.1 The objectives of IPC

The main objectives of IPC are:

- to prevent or minimize the release of prescribed substances and to render harmless any such substances that are released;
- to develop an approach to pollution control that considers discharges from industrial processes to all media in the context of the environment as a whole.

4.2 Industrial processes affected by IPC

IPC applies to any industrial process carried out in England or Wales which has been prescribed by the Secretary of State for the Environment.

The processes (in the sense that they are controlled by specific regulations) prescribed are listed in the Environmental Protection (Prescribed Processes and Substances) Regulations 1991. Anyone intending to carry out one of these processes must make an application to the Environment Agency, giving full details of the process. The Environment Agency will then assess the effects on the environment as a whole and, if necessary, will require the applicant to modify the process, making it less polluting.

Before authorization is granted, various statutory objectives have to be met. Account has to be taken of emissions to all three media: land, water and air.

The Environmental Protection (Applications, Appeals and Registers) Regulations 1991 describe the application procedures.

EXTENSION 9
The main prescribed processes are listed on page 101 of this workbook.

Some examples of the processes listed in the Regulations are:

■ petrochemical processes and acid manufacturing processes in the chemical industry;

■ asbestos processes and fibre processes in the minerals industry;

■ iron and steel processes and smelting processes in the minerals industry.

4.3 Prescribed substances

Normally, controlling a prescribed process will result in the control of any noxious substance emitted. However, there are also Regulations that specifically apply to the release of prescribed substances. Examples of these include:

Releases into the air:	Oxides of sulphur and other sulphur compounds. Metals, metalloids and their compounds. Asbestos and glass fibres.
Releases into water:	Mercury and its compounds. Cadmium and its compounds. Polychlorinated biphenyls (PCBs).
Releases to land:	Organic solvents. Phosphorus. Pesticides.

As you will discover when we discuss water pollution, there are other kinds of pollution that are dealt with separately.

4.4 BATNEEC

Under integrated pollution control, the principle of **BATNEEC – best available technique not entailing excessive cost** is employed.

What does this mean? Suppose a manufacturer is carrying out one of the prescribed processes. It may be possible to reduce the pollution from the process by employing better techniques or equipment. It would then be up to the organization to prove that the costs of these new techniques or equipment would outweigh the benefits they would bring. Even if the

Environment Agency agree, the organization may still be required to phase in the new equipment over a period of time.

No prescribed process can be carried out and no substance emitted without authorization from the appropriate Environment Agency. Anyone carrying out a prescribed process without authorization **will be guilty of a criminal offence**.

5 How the law is enforced

There are a number of official bodies involved in environmental protection. We will take a brief look at some of the most important ones and discuss their different roles and functions.

5.1 The Environment Agency for England and Wales, and the Scottish Environment Protection Agency

These Environment Agencies, as we have already seen, are tasked with implementing an integrated and coherent approach to pollution control and have overall responsibility for doing this. The Agency has responsibility for the regulation of pollution for most hazardous activities, including:

- operating the system of integrated pollution control (IPC);
- control of radioactive substances;
- monitoring waste disposal;
- control of air pollution;
- control of water pollution.

5.2 Sewage undertakers

The licensing body for controlling discharges to sewers is the privatized sewage undertaker, which is able to grant permission for industrial discharges, called 'trade effluent consents'. This is an unusual case of a private organization taking on the role of regulation of pollution. Appeals go to the Director General of Water Services.

5.3 Local authorities

Local authorities have responsibilities for a number of environmental matters:

■ Town and country planning

The local authority is normally the local planning authority. It also has responsibility for conservation areas, listed building protection and protection of the countryside.

■ Waste disposal

County councils are the waste disposal authorities, and are the bodies that deal with waste disposal applications.

■ Public health

Local authorities have wide powers under the Public Health Acts, including control of nuisances, noise and litter.

■ Air pollution

Local authorities have responsibility for control of smoke, fumes, dust, etc.

5.4 Prosecution and punishment

Traditionally, the 'British approach' to enforcement of environmental laws has been one of 'co-operation rather than confrontation'. This attitude stems from the belief that the main aim of pollution control is to prevent harm to the environment or harm to humans, rather than to detect and punish.

Until fairly recently, the regulatory bodies were very reluctant to use the ultimate sanction of prosecution and punishment under the law. Most pollution offences are the result of accidents, and the enforcers have placed more emphasis on the intention of the polluters, rather than the offences themselves. Only when companies have seemed to deliberately and persistently flout the law have stronger measures been taken.

However, the EU has placed regulatory bodies under increasing pressure to prosecute offenders. Public opinion also supports this approach. The Environment Agency, and its immediate predecessors HMIP (Her Majesty's Inspectorate of Pollution) and the NRA (National Rivers Authority), have shown that they intend taking a stronger line.

Activity 29

2 mins

How has your organization reacted to the way in which the law is now being enforced?

_____

_____

In general terms it seems that companies and other organizations are having to take much more care in preventing pollution and protecting the environment if they are to avoid prosecution.

5.5 The powers of inspectors under IPC

Under the system of integrated pollution control, the Environment Agency for England and Wales and the Scottish Environment Protection Agency both have very wide powers. If you scan through the following list you will get an idea of just how much power the law has given to environmental inspectors, who may:

- enter premises; although this is usually done at a reasonable time, entry can be made at any time where there is a risk of serious pollution;
- examine and investigate any process contained in any premises;
- direct that any premises and items contained in those premises remain undisturbed;
- take measurements, photographs and make recordings;
- take samples of air, water, articles or substances on or in the vicinity of the premises;
- require any articles or substances to be dismantled or subjected to any process or test;
- take possession and detain any article or substance;
- require persons to answer questions if the inspector reasonably believes them to be able to give relevant information and, once they have supplied answers, to sign a declaration as to the truth of those answers;
- require the production of any records;
- require the provision of any substance or facilities necessary to carry out any of the duties mentioned above;
- seize and render harmless any article or substance which is believed to be the cause of imminent danger.

6 The law on waste management

Some 500,000,000 tonnes of waste are produced annually in Britain; this figure gives some indication of the size of the waste management problem. Waste comes from domestic premises, industry, farms, mines, quarries, sewage, power stations and other sources.

Activity 30

2 mins

Write down at least **one** difficulty associated with the disposal of waste from your own workplace.

_____

_____

Most waste is disposed of in large holes in the ground – so-called landfill sites. The main problem with doing this is that many substances break down over a period of time and create hazardous substances, thus polluting the land and nearby water environments. Other methods of disposal include incineration and dumping at sea, both these methods have their problems.

The Environmental Protection Act, 1990 introduced a new system of waste management, and placed a 'duty of care' on all businesses to prevent improper disposal of waste. Under the EPA:

> Controlled waste is any household, commercial or industrial waste, such as waste from a house, shop, office, factory, building site or any other business premises.

'any business which produces, imports, stores, treats, processes, transports, recycles or disposes of controlled waste must, by law, take all reasonable steps to look after any waste it has and prevent its illegal disposal by others'.

When waste changes hands, a transfer note must be completed and signed by both parties and a written description of the waste handed over. (This does not apply to household waste.)

7 The law on water pollution

The water environment comprises rivers, streams, natural and artificial lakes, underground waters and coastal areas.

Activity 31 · 3 mins

How many sources of water pollution can you think of? For instance, one source is industrial discharge by factories. Try to list **two** others.

_____

_____

_____

_____

Besides industrial emissions, you might have mentioned:

■ Farms

Fertilizers or silage plants sometimes leach into nearby streams and rivers; this gives rise to a process called **eutrophication** in which the nitrates and phosphates in these materials cause an excessive growth of algae. Pesticides and herbicides may also find their way into water courses from farms.

■ Sewage works

Many sewage works have consent to discharge their contents directly into coastal waters and other water environments.

■ Waste sites

Natural rain can cause leaching of noxious materials from waste tips.

■ Mines

The waste waters from mines may contaminate water courses.

■ Accidents

If chemicals or other substances are being transported and an accident occurs, they may flow directly into rivers or lakes.

■ People

It isn't unknown for people to throw away unwanted rubbish into rivers, streams and canals.

7.1 The system of 'consents'

If an organization wants to discharge trade or sewage effluent into any inland or coastal waters, it can only do so when given a consent by the Environment Agency for England and Wales, or the Scottish Environment Protection Agency. Trade effluents includes discharge from farms, fish farms or from industrial plants. A consent also has to be granted before any discharge is made through pipes into the sea.

It is an offence to 'cause or knowingly permit' any such discharge unless it is carried out with a consent.

The 'polluter pays' principle applies and all costs by the enforcing agency will be recovered from the organization making the discharge.

7.2 The new water companies

Under the Water Act 1989 the regional water authorities were privatized. Ten water services companies were set up, having responsibility for water supply and sewage services. Twenty-nine other smaller ones are responsible for water supply only.

Although the Water Act 1989 set up the new structure for the industry, it was replaced in December 1991 by five new Acts. These made hardly any change to the law, however. The new Acts are the:

■ Water Industry Act 1991;
■ Water Resources Act 1991;
■ Water Companies Act 1991;
■ Land Drainage Act 1991;
■ Water Consolidation (Consequential and Amendments) Act 1991.

8 The law on atmospheric pollution

Air is essential for humans and most other land creatures. Pollution of the air can have devastating consequences.

Activity 32

3 mins

Which industries would you expect to be the worst air polluters?

_____

_____

_____

_____

List **two** or **three** substances that are pumped into the atmosphere by industry, and which are considered as being detrimental to the environment.

_____

_____

_____

_____

Many types of industry use processes that discharge undesirable substances. The power generation industry is one that is commonly focused upon, because it is so large, and burns so much fuel.

For example, over a period of five years, the average thermal efficiency of coal-burning stations of one national company was raised from 35.37 per cent to 36.10 per cent. This does not seem to be a great improvement, until you realize that the saving reduced coal consumption by 800,000 tonnes, and cut carbon dioxide emissions by over 2 million tonnes.

Apart from carbon dioxide, which contributes to global warming, other substances emitted by power stations and factories burning coal and oil include:

- carbon monoxide;
- sulphur dioxide;
- nitric oxide;
- nitrogen dioxide;
- nitrous oxide;
- hydrochloric acid;
- particulate material;
- mercury.

Problems of air pollution have been written about since at least the seventeenth century, but with the coming of the industrial revolution the problems grew worse. The universal adoption of coal as a fuel meant that the smoking chimney became the symbol of industry. Acid emissions from caustic soda factories caused the first acid rain.

The effects on the countryside surrounding industrial towns were devastating: often trees just could not survive. Smog was commonplace from Victorian times. The effects of breathing this polluted atmosphere can be imagined.

Just as private cars are major polluters of the atmosphere, so domestic fires were responsible for much of the air pollution which led to smogs in most large cities and towns. Central heating and air conditioning systems now account for substantial amounts of pollution. They do so directly through the domestic burning of fossil fuels, and indirectly by increasing the demand for electricity generated by power stations.

8.1 Control of smoke

The Clean Air Acts of 1956 and 1968 provided a control mechanism for smoke, dust and fumes. These Acts prohibited the emission of 'dark smoke' from the chimney of any building, whether domestic or industrial; offenders were guilty of a criminal offence.

The height of chimneys was also brought under control in the 1968 Act. The idea was to increase the height of chimneys so as to disperse emissions over a wider area.

Activity 33

3 mins

What effects do you think that simply increasing the height of chimneys had on the environment?

_____

_____

_____

Unless something is done about the problem of the emissions themselves, increasing chimney heights simply spreads the pollution over a wider area. This may alleviate the local problem but, as is now recognized, passes on the pollution to another area or another country.

8.2 Air pollution control

The Environmental Protection Act 1990 introduced a system of air pollution control (APC).

APC is a similar system to IPC (integrated pollution control) but covers only the less polluting substances, and is controlled by local authorities rather than the environment agencies. It includes:

- lower grade combustion processes;
- small iron and steel furnaces;
- low grade waste incineration;
- animal and vegetable treatment processes.

As with IPC, anyone carrying out a prescribed process or emitting a prescribed substance that is subject to air pollution control must have an authorization to do so. It is a criminal offence to break this law.

8.3 The control of vehicle emissions

The emission of pollutants from road vehicles is controlled by the Road Traffic Act 1988 together with regulations relating to the construction of vehicles and type approval.

The regulations have been changed regularly to take account of EU Directives, such as those on carbon monoxide emissions.

All cars manufactured after 1 October 1989 have had to be capable of running on unleaded petrol.

All cars with an engine size over 1000 cc manufactured from 1992 onwards have had to be fitted with a three-way catalytic converter. This device is fitted to the exhaust of the vehicle, and considerably reduces polluting emissions. Catalytic converters can only be used with unleaded petrol.

However, much of this gain has been offset by increased numbers of cars and increased numbers of journeys in them, for both business and pleasure.

Self-assessment 3

20 mins.

1 Explain briefly what is meant by the principle of 'the polluter pays'.

_____

_____

_____

2 What are the **four** principal areas of environmental law?

_____

_____

_____

_____

3 Fill in the blanks in the following statements with suitable words.

The main objectives of IPC are:

■ to prevent or minimize the release of _____ _____

and to render _____ any such substances which are released;

■ to develop an approach to _____ control that considers

discharges from _____ processes to all media in the context of

the _____ as a whole.

4   Explain briefly what BATNEEC (best available technique not entailing excessive cost) means.

_____

_____

_____

5   Which of the following statements are correct? Tick the correct ones.

a   The Environment Agency for England and Wales, or the Scottish Environment Protection Agency, have the right to bring an organization's work to a complete halt. ☐

b   One of the key policies of new legislation is the lowering of chimney heights. ☐

c   Among the list of industrial air pollutants are nitric oxide; nitrous oxide; and hydrochloric acid. ☐

d   Under no circumstances would sewage works obtain consent to discharge their contents directly into water environments. ☐

e   One problem with dumping waste on landfill sites is that many substances break down over a period of time and create hazardous substances, thus polluting land and water environments. ☐

f   It is acceptable for organizations to pollute the environment, provided they pay for clearing up the mess afterwards. ☐

Answers to these questions can be found on pages 104–5.

9 Summary

■ Environmental law has undergone some radical changes in the last 20 years or so.

■ Like health and safety, environmental law typically consists of framework Acts, which give rise to Regulations that spell out the detail.

■ The environmental policies of the EU have already greatly influenced British environmental legislation, and are likely to continue to do so in the future. The basic principles of these policies are that:

   ■ preventative action is to be preferred to remedial measures;
   ■ environmental damage should be rectified at source;
   ■ the polluter should pay for the costs of the measures taken to protect the environment;
   ■ environmental policies should form a component of the EU's other policies.

■ The four principal areas of environmental law are:

   ■ pollution;
   ■ water;
   ■ nature conservation;
   ■ town and country planning.

■ Recent legislation includes the Environmental Protection Act 1990 (EPA), and the Environment Act, 1995.

■ The main objectives of integrated pollution control (IPC) are:

   ■ to prevent or minimize the release of prescribed substances and to render harmless any such substances which are released;
   ■ to develop an approach to pollution control that considers discharges from industrial processes to all media in the context of the environment as a whole.

■ Under integrated pollution control, the principle of BATNEEC – best available technique not entailing excessive cost – is employed.

■ The main enforcement agency is the Environment Agency for England and Wales. In Scotland it is the Scottish Environment Protection Agency. Both have very wide powers, and are under pressure from the EU to prosecute offenders.

■ The Environmental Protection Act 1990 introduced a new system of waste management, and placed a 'duty of care' on all businesses to prevent improper disposal of waste.

■ If any organization wants to discharge any trade or sewage effluent into any inland or coastal waters, it can only do so when given a consent by one of the two environment agencies.

■ The Environmental Protection Act 1990 introduced a system of air pollution control (APC). APC is a similar system to IPC (integrated pollution control) but covers only the less polluting substances, and is controlled by local authorities rather than the environment agencies.

Performance checks

1 Quick quiz

Jot down the answers to the following questions on *Managing Lawfully – Health, Safety and Environment*:

Question 1   What do you understand by the term 'enabling law'? Give two examples.

_____

_____

_____

Question 2   What are the **three** routes by which an organization might have a legal action brought against it, as a result of an accident at work?

_____

_____

_____

Question 3   When a Directive is issued by the EU, what actions are taken by member States?

_____

_____

Question 4   One thing an employer must do, in order to comply with HSWA, is to ensure plant and equipment are safely installed, operated and maintained. Give **two** other examples of what it must do.

_____

_____

Question 5   How would you summarize the responsibilities of employees under HSWA?

_____

_____

Question 6   If a regulation uses the words 'the employer shall', how should that be interpreted?

_____

_____

Question 7   How would you explain what it means to carry out a risk assessment, in a sentence or two?

_____

_____

Question 8   Briefly, what is the purpose of health surveillance?

_____

_____

Question 9   How would you define a 'competent person' who is to help an employer comply with health and safety laws?

_____

_____

Question 10   Which **two** sets of regulations are important in respect of workstations?

_____

_____

Question 11   What's the first thing you should consider, if you plan to move a heavy load manually?

_____

_____

Question 12   List **two** requirements for employers under the Personal Protective Equipment at Work Regulations 1992 (PPEWR).

_____

_____

Question 13   How would you define a hazardous substance, under COSHH?

_____

_____

Question 14   Write down **one** of the four EU basic policy principles in respect of environmental legislation.

_____

_____

Question 15   What must an organization do before it discharges any trade or sewage effluent into inland or coastal waters?

_____

_____

Question 16   Name three ways in which an organization can cause harm to its local environment.

_____

_____

Question 17   How can an organization help to protect its staff against malicious attack by members of the public?

_____

_____

Question 18   List four injuries that are defined as 'major injuries' under RIDDOR and one 'dangerous occurrence'.

_____

_____

Question 19   Name two important requirements imposed by the Fire Precautions Act.

_____

_____

Question 20   Quote one responsibility each of (i) senior management and (ii) all employees under a Health and Safety Policy that would comply with HSWA.

_____

_____

Answers to these questions can be found on pages 105–7.

2 Workbook assessment

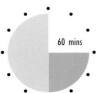

60 mins

Anne and Peter Haydock are converting a water mill into a tea room and souvenir shop. They hope to attract parents and children as customers. The mill wheel is being restored to working condition and will be maintained by a specialist contractor. Visitors will be able to enter some mill buildings and enjoy walking by the mill stream, pool and race, which attract wild fowl and small animals.

It is now two weeks before the scheduled opening day and various contractors are still working on site. They all say they will be finished in time, but Anne doubts it. This worries her. So does a newspaper report of an HSE prosecution of a similar business where a young customer was seriously injured during building work which wasn't screened off.

The Haydocks know that you have been studying the Law in these areas. They have asked you to advise them urgently on how to meet their legal obligations towards:

■ employees (of whom there will be six, carrying out work relating to the tea room, shop, general cleaning and routine maintenance);
■ the general public and delivery personnel;
■ contractors' employees who will be working there from time to time, including window cleaners for the upper floors, millwrights, maintenance staff for catering equipment, and so on;
■ the environment, especially regarding pollution and litter.

Design a simple check list that the Haydocks can use to check that they will be managing their new business lawfully.

Your checklist should cover the four areas they have indicated. It should tell them simply what their obligations are and list the main Acts and Regulations which you believe could apply to each.

Think carefully through the implications for their business of HSWA and EPA generally and Regulations such as COSHH, Electricity at Work, PUWER and MHSWR.

Don't go into too much detail. Try to deal with the main principles of law aimed at protecting the safety of people and the environment.

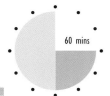
60 mins

3 Work-based assignment

Portfolio of evidence

S/NVQ A1.2

The time guide for this assignment gives you an approximate idea of how long it is likely to take you to write up your findings. You will find you need to spend some additional time gathering information, talking to colleagues, and thinking about the assignment.

Your written response to this assignment may form useful evidence for your S/NVQ portfolio. The assignment is designed to help you to demonstrate your Personal Competence in:

■ building teams;
■ focusing on results;
■ thinking and taking decisions.

What you have to do

Select one of the Regulations we discussed in the workbook, and carry out a brief investigation into how well your part of the organization complies with it. A good start might be to look at a recent accident or, better still, any 'near miss' statistics you have available for the area you work in. Once you have decided which Regulation deserves priority treatment, start by drawing up a checklist. Then, by talking with your team and other colleagues, and by making observations, decide whether (and, if appropriate, how well) the law is being complied with.

Once you have done that, decide what steps need to be taken in order to ensure that any areas that are falling short of full compliance (or failing altogether) can be brought up to scratch.

Write up your findings and recommendations in the form of a report to your manager.

Reflect and review

1 Reflect and review

Now that you have completed your work on *Managing Lawfully – Health, Safety and Environment*, let us review our workbook objectives.

The first objective was:

■ When you have completed this workbook you will be better able to identify the most important laws related to health and safety.

We have covered a lot of ground in this workbook: many different statutes related to health and safety were reviewed. These are the laws that are currently the most important to work organizations generally.

  ■ What can you do to increase your knowledge of health and safety law?

  _____

  _____

The second objective was:

■ When you have completed this workbook you will be better able to find out more about laws that are especially relevant to the work you do.

If you followed the workbook carefully, you should now have at least some idea about the kind of laws that deal with your type of work and organization. Now's the time to follow these up.

■ Write down the laws that you know about, that are particularly relevant to your work.

_____

_____

_____

_____

_____

_____

_____

■ Now write down the actions you plan to take to find out more about these and (perhaps) other laws.

_____

_____

_____

_____

_____

_____

_____

The third objective was:

■ When you have completed this workbook you will be better able to explain to your team how the law affects them, and the duties imposed by the law on everyone at work.

A good starting point would be the Health and Safety at Work, etc. Act 1974, which makes specific reference to employees' duties. Then you should consider the other 'six-pack' regulations, and COSHH if relevant, all of which we covered in Session B.

■ Are you clear in your own mind about these laws, at least so far as to be able to pass on the relevant information?

_____

_____

■ If you are still confused about the law, what steps do you intend to take to clarify your thinking on the subject?

_____

_____

■ If your team is in need of further information and training on health and safety, what plans will you make for them to receive it?

_____

_____

The final objective was:

■ When you have completed this workbook you will be better able to understand the law on the environment.

Session C was concerned with environmental law. We took a brief look at the four aspects of the environment: water, pollution; nature conservation; and town and country planning. In addition, we discussed the two main laws: the Environmental Protection Act 1990, and the Environment Act 1995, and mentioned a number of others.

Like health and safety law, environmental law imposes a great number of requirements on organizations and employers. To a large extent, the law reflects public concern over these issues. So, again in common with health and safety, it is not usually enough simply to comply with the law. The public image of an organization can deteriorate dramatically if it is not seen to be taking a constructive attitude, and taking positive actions.

■ Be honest: how well do you understand environmental law, at least so far as it affects your activities at work?

_____

_____

■ What steps do you intend to take to increase your knowledge and awareness of environmental issues?

_____

_____

2 Action plan

Use this plan to further develop for yourself a course of action you want to take. Make a note in the left-hand column of the issues or problems you want to tackle, and then decide what you intend to do, and make a note in column 2.

The resources you need might include time, materials, information or money. You may need to negotiate for some of them, but they could be something easily acquired, like half an hour of somebody's time, or a chapter of a book. Put whatever you need in column 3. No plan means anything without a timescale, so put a realistic target completion date in column 4.

Finally, describe the outcome you want to achieve as a result of this plan, whether it is for your own benefit or advancement, or a more efficient way of doing things.

Desired outcomes				
1 Issues	2 Action	3 Resources	4 Target completion	
Actual outcomes				

3 Extensions

Extension 1	Book	*Health and Safety Law*
	Author	Jeremy Stranks
	Edition	4th edition 2001
	Publisher	Prentice Hall

Extension 2	Book	*Workplace health, safety and welfare: a short guide for managers*
	Edition	1997
	Publisher	HSE Books

Available from the HSE website: www.hsebooks.co.uk

Extension 3	Book	*Successful health and safety management*
	Edition	1997
	Publisher	HSE Books

Available from the HSE website: www.hsebooks.co.uk

Extension 4	Book	*Safety representatives and safety committees*
	Edition	1996
	Publisher	HSE Books

Available from the HSE website: www.hsebooks.co.uk

Extension 5	Book	*Management of Health and Safety at Work Regulations 1999 Approved Code of Practice and guidance*
	Edition	2000
	Publisher	HSE Books

Available from the HSE website: www.hsebooks.co.uk

Extension 6	Book	*Manual Handling Operations Regulations 1999*
	Edition	1998
	Publisher	HSE Books

Available from the HSE website: www.hsebooks.co.uk

Extension 7	Book	*VDUs: an easy guide to the Regulations. How to comply with the Health and Safety (display screen equipment) Regulations 1992*
	Edition	1997
	Publisher	HSE Books

Available from the HSE website: www.hsebooks.co.uk

Extension 8   COMPANY _____

HEALTH & SAFETY DATA RECORD

SECTION 1 – PRODUCT IDENTIFICATION

TRADE NAME/CHEMICAL NAME	
APPROX. ANNUAL CONSUMPTION	
SUPPLIER/MANUFACTURER	
STORAGE AREA	
POINT (S) OF USE	

SECTION 2 – HAZARDOUS INGREDIENTS

MATERIAL OR COMPONENT	

SECTION 3 – PHYSICAL PROPERTIES

APPEARANCE AND COLOUR		
SPECIFIC GRAVITY ($H_2O = 1$)	**SOLUBILITY IN WATER:**	
BULK DENSITY:	**VISCOSITY AT:**	**pH 1% SOLN:**

SECTION 4 – FLAMMABILITY & EXPLOSIVE PROPERTIES

FLASH POINT (TEST METHOD)	
EXTINGUISHING MEDIA	
SPECIAL FIRE FIGHTING PROCEDURES	
UNUSUAL FIRE & EXPLOSION HAZARD	

SECTION 5 – HEALTH HAZARD DATA   REPORT *ALL* ACCIDENTS TO THE SURGERY

THRESHOLD LIMIT VALUE	
EFFECTS OF EXPOSURE	
EMERGENCY FIRST AID PROCEDURES **EYES:** **SKIN:** **INGESTION:** **INHALATION:**	

SECTION 6 – REACTIVE DATA

STABLE:	CONDITIONS TO AVOID:	
MATERIALS TO AVOID		
HAZARDOUS DECOMPOSITION PRODUCTS		

SECTION 7 – SPILL OR LEAK PROCEDURES

STEPS TO TAKE IN CASE MATERIALS RELEASED OR SPILLED	
WASTE DISPOSAL METHOD	

SECTION 8 – SPECIAL PROTECTION INFORMATION

TYPE OF RESPIRATORY EQUIPMENT	
VENTILATION	
LOCAL EXHAUST: MECHANICAL GEN:	SPECIAL (SPECIFY): OTHER (SPECIFY):
PROTECTIVE GLOVES:	EYE PROTECTION:
OTHER PROTECTIVE EQUIPMENT	

SECTION 9 – SPECIAL PRECAUTIONS

HANDLING & STORAGE PRECAUTIONS	
OTHER PRECAUTIONS	

PREPARED BY:	TIME:	DATE:
SITE AUTHORIZATION:		DATE:

Extension 9   List of prescribed processes affected by integrated pollution control.

Mineral Industry

Cement
Asbestos
Fibre
Glass
Ceramic

Fuel and Power Industry

Combustion (>50MWth):
boilers and furnaces
Gasification
Carbonization
Combustion (remainder)
Petroleum

Chemical Industry

Petrochemical
Organic
Chemical pesticide
Pharmaceutical
Acid manufacturing
Halogen
Chemical fertilizer
Bulk chemical storage
Inorganic material

Waste Disposal Industry

Incineration
Chemical recovery
Waste-derived fuel

Other Industry

Paper manufacturing
Di-isocyanate
Tar and bitumen
Uranium
Coating
Coating manufacturing
Timber
Animal and plant treatment

Metal Industry

Iron and steel
Smelting
Non-ferrous

4 Answers to self-assessment questions

Self-assessment 1 on pages 27–8

1   The correct statements are:

b   Contract law is relatively unimportant in health and safety matters.

c   Following an accident, an organization may be prosecuted under either criminal law or civil law.

d   European law takes precedence over UK law.

f   The Health and Safety at Work, etc. Act 1974, places an obligation on employers to take care of the health and safety of customers on its premises.

g   Employees have duties to co-operate with employers in meeting the requirements of the law.

i   'As far as reasonably practicable' means that the degree of risk can be balanced against the cost of taking measures to avoid the risk.

2   Safety representatives may be involved in:

■ TALKING to employees about particular health and safety problems;

■ encouraging CO-OPERATION between their employer and employees;

■ carrying out INSPECTIONS of the workplace to see whether there are any real or potential HAZARDS that haven't been adequately addressed;

■ bringing to the attention of the employer any UNSAFE or unhealthy conditions or working PRACTICES, or unsatisfactory WELFARE arrangements;

■ REPORTING to employers about these problems and other matters connected to health and safety in that WORKPLACE;

■ taking part in ACCIDENT investigations.

3   a   Approved codes of practice (ACOPs) – [vii] Issued by the Health and Safety Commission (HSC) as interpretations of regulations, and are intended to help people apply the law in practice.

b   Civil law – [iv] A plaintiff sues a defendant, usually for damages, that is, financial compensation. As an example, an individual may sue an employer if he or she is injured at work.

c Prohibition notice – [ii] stops, with immediate effect, prople from carrying out activities that are considered to involved a risk of serious personal injury.

d Criminal law – [iii] Anyone committing a crime has offended against the state, and is in breach of this. If an organization fails to comply with its statutory health and safety duties, its officers may be prosecuted.

e EU Directives – [vi] Bind member countries to comply with an agreed ruling. They are normally made into national laws by each state.

f Improvement notice – [v] compels an employer to put right conditions that contravene the health and safety law.

g Statute law – [i] Acts of Parliament (such as the Health and Safety at Work, etc. Act 1974), together with a great many 'statutory instruments' or 'subordinate legislation'.

Self-assessment 2 on pages 60–1	1 **Under MHSWR, employers must:**	**This includes the process of:**
	a provide risk assessment	iii identifying the hazard; measuring and evaluating the risk from this hazard; putting measures into place that will either eliminate the hazard, or control it
	b provide health surveillance	i identifying adverse affects; rectifying inadequacies in control; informing those at risk of any damage to their health; reinforcing health education
	c appoint competent persons	iv identifying those with sufficient training, and experience or knowledge and other qualities; requiring them to devise and apply the measures needed to comply with health and safety laws
	d consult employees' safety representatives	ii identifying measures that may substantially affect health and safety; identifying health and safety aspects of new technology; discussing these with the relevant people.

2 More than one regulation will apply in most work situations. Some you may have identified are as follows.

i Loading bags of flour: [c] Manual Handling Operations Regulations 1992 (MHOR).

ii Supervising telesales: [d] Health and Safety (Display Screen Equipment) Regulations 1992.

iii Running an electrical department in a superstore: [b] Workplace (Health, Safety and Welfare) Regulations 1992 (WHSWR).

iv Training fork-lift truck drivers in a fuel depot: [a] Management of Health and Safety at Work Regulations 1999 (MHSWR).

v Supervising an area where there are high levels of dust. [a] Management of Health and Safety at Work Regulations 1992 (MHSWR),

vi Supervising on a building site: [e] Personal Protective Equipment at Work (PPE) Regulations 1992 (PPEWR).

3 Under the COSHH regulations, employers have to:

■ determine the HAZARD of SUBSTANCES used by the organization;

■ assess the RISK to people's health from the way the substances are used;

■ prevent anyone being EXPOSED to the substances, if possible;

■ if exposure cannot be prevented, decide how to CONTROL the exposure so as to reduce the risk, and then establish effective CONTROLS;

■ ensure that the controls are properly used and MAINTAINED;

■ examine and TEST the control measures, if this is required;

■ inform, INSTRUCT and train employees (and non-employees on the premises), so that they are aware of the hazards and how to work SAFELY;

■ if necessary, MONITOR the exposure of employees (and non-employees on the premises), and provide HEALTH SURVEILLANCE to employees if necessary.

Self-assessment 3 on pages 84–5

1 The principle of the polluter pays means that producers of goods or services should be responsible for the costs of preventing or dealing with any pollution that they may cause.

2 The four principal areas of environmental law are:

■ pollution;

■ water;

■ nature conservation;

■ town and country planning.

3 The main objectives of IPC are:

■ to prevent or minimize the release of **prescribed substances** and to render **harmless** any such substances which are released;

■ to develop an approach to **pollution** control that considers discharges from **industrial** processes to all media in the context of the **environment** as a whole.

4   BATNEEC means that organizations must use the best available techniques in reducing or eliminating pollution, unless they can prove that the costs of these techniques would outweigh the benefits.

5   The correct statements are as follows.

a   The Environment Agency for England and Wales, or the Scottish Environment Protection Agency, have the right to bring an organization's work to a complete halt.

c   Among the list of industrial air pollutants are nitric oxide; nitrous oxide; and hydrochloric acid.

e   One problem with dumping waste on landfill sites is that many substances break down over a period of time and create hazardous substances, thus polluting land and water environments.

5 Answers to the quick quiz

Answer 1   Enabling Acts allow (or 'enable') Ministers to issue detailed Regulations at a later date, without the need to have them debated in full in Parliament. Examples are the Health and Safety at Work, etc. Act 1974 (HSWA) and the Environment Protection Act EPA).

Answer 2   The two main routes are through the civil and criminal courts. The third route is via an employment tribunal.

Answer 3   Directives, which bind member countries to comply with an agreed ruling, are normally made into national laws by each state.

Answer 4   Other examples are: check systems of work frequently to ensure that risks from hazards are minimized; monitor the work environment regularly, to ensure that people are protected from any toxic contaminants; inspect safety equipment regularly; minimize risks to health from 'natural and artificial substances'.

Answer 5   Employees have responsibilities under HSWA to take care for their own health and safety, and that of their colleagues; to co-operate in meeting the requirements of the law including the acceptance of health and safety training; not to interfere with or misuse anything provided to protect their health, safety and welfare.

Answer 6   If the words 'the employer shall' are used, it means that the requirement that follows is compulsory.

Answer 7   To carry out a risk assessment, you must identify the hazard; measure and evaluate the risk from this hazard; and put measures into place that will either eliminate the hazard, or control it.

Answer 8   The purpose of health surveillance is to identify adverse affects early; rectify inadequacies in control, and so reduce the risks to those affected or exposed; inform those at risk, as soon as possible, of any damage to their health, so that they can take action; and to reinforce health education.

Answer 9   A person can be regarded as competent if he or she has 'sufficient training, and experience or knowledge and other qualities, properly to undertake' the role.

Answer 10   The Workplace (Health, Safety and Welfare) Regulations 1992 (WHSWR), and the Health and Safety (Display Screen Equipment) Regulations 1992.

Answer 11   You should consider whether the load must be moved at all, and if so, whether it could be moved by non-manual methods.

Answer 12   Under PPEWR, employers have to ensure this equipment is suitable and appropriate; maintain, clean and replace it; provide storage for it when not in use; ensure that it is properly used; give employees training, information and instruction in its use.

Answer 13   A hazardous substance is virtually any substance in the workplace.

Answer 14   The basic principles of EU environmental policies are that: preventative action is to be preferred to remedial measures; environmental damage should be rectified at source; the polluter should pay for the costs of the measures taken to protect the environment; environmental policies should form a component of the EU's other policies.

Answer 15   The organization must obtain a consent.

Answer 16   Three ways in which an organization can cause harm to its local environment are by:

- burning rubbish on bonfires or in incinerators;
- poring fats or chemicals down drains;
- allowing building contractors to 'fly tip' hazardous waste materials such as asbestos.

Answer 17   Organizations can protect their staff from malicious attack by:

- training them how to recognize potentially violent people;
- training them how to defuse the situation where possible;
- providing emergency help systems where essential for their safety.

Answer 18   Examples of injuries defined as 'major injuries' under RIDDOR include death, fractured skull, amputation and loss of sight. An example of a 'dangerous occurrence' would be an explosion or fire which stopped work for 24 hours or more.

Answer 19   The Fire Precautions Act requires that:

- a specified means of escape must be provided (and kept clear at all times)
- fire fighting equipment that must be provided and maintained.

Answer 20   The Health and Safety Policy must specify that:

(i) senior management must review and update the Policy and provide sufficient resources to implement it;
(ii) all personnel must take reasonable care for the health and safety of themselves, colleagues and other people who may be affected by their actions.

6 Certificate

Completion of this certificate by an authorized person shows that you have worked through all the parts of this workbook and satisfactorily completed the assessments. The certificate provides a record of what you have done that may be used for exemptions or as evidence of prior learning against other nationally certificated qualifications.

Pergamon Flexible Learning and ILM are always keen to refine and improve their products. One of the key sources of information to help this process are people who have just used the product. If you have any information or views, good or bad, please pass these on.

INSTITUTE OF LEADERSHIP & MANAGEMENT

SUPERSERIES

Managing Lawfully –
Health, Safety and Environment

....

has satisfactorily completed this workbook

Name of signatory   ....

Position   ....

Signature   ....

Date   ....

Official stamp

Fourth Edition

INSTITUTE OF LEADERSHIP & MANAGEMENT
SUPERSERIES
FOURTH EDITION

To order – phone us direct for prices and availability details
(please quote ISBNs when ordering) on 01865 888190